ENDURING POWER

D1150150

RON McCATTY

ARTHUR H. STOCKWELL LTD.
Elms Court   Ilfracombe
Devon

*All Bible quotations are
taken from the A.V. unless
otherwise stated.*

ISBN 0 7223 1638-0
Printed in Great Britain by
Arthur H. Stockwell Ltd.
Elms Court   Ilfracombe
Devon

CONTENTS

CHAPTER ONE

THE FREE GIFT

"Be filled with the Spirit." This is the command of Ephesians 5:18.

Not only are we required to be filled with, but to 'walk in' and 'live in the Spirit'. A tall order! No! It is only a matter of letting go and letting God take over our lives. He wants to bless and promote us. We can only prosper under His management.

We live in a world of power seekers. Numerous men and women projecting their personalities strive for mastery, for independence, for dominance. Money, education, politics, music, philosophy . . . enjoy pride of place in our societies as keys to power: and to what end! In the final analysis, really nothing of any eternal value.

In the Christian sense there is a much higher, and far more enduring power, God's power: 'power from on high' as the Bible puts it. Jesus has promised that this power shall be conferred upon us from heaven. Free, elevating, strengthening — it is a hedge against delusion, for in effect it is really a matter of being filled with God.

He said we shall receive this, after that the Holy Ghost is come upon us, and we shall be witnesses unto

5

Him (Acts 1:8).

Who would not like being a witness unto Jesus?

This does not mean that after receiving the Holy Spirit in this particular way we shall become just better talkers about our Saviour.

We may well become more vocal, yes, but words are not enough. They must be backed up by supernatural works. They must bear fruit that reflect the very nature of God, the giver of that power. Jesus Himself received a powerful anointing from His Heavenly Father and His witnessing was with miracles, signs and wonders. 'We are witnesses of all things which He did . . .' (Acts 10:39). Witnesses! Surely this suggests that we are not only admirers, onlookers, or speakers, but demonstrators of His life and works. In fact, God intends that we should have the same anointing that was upon Jesus. So the Bible says 'we are joint heirs with Christ'.

Therefore, however Pentecostal our preaching or teaching might be, without the supernatural that was present in Jesus' ministry, and in that of the Early Church, there is no evidence of the Baptism in the Holy Spirit.

The disciples were all filled with the Spirit. They knew Him in an intimate way. He was the very solution to their need as they stood bereft of their Leader and Friend, Jesus, who had been slain.

Through the ministry of the Holy Spirit empowered Church the Gospel was destined to reach the uttermost parts of the earth. His ministry has not changed. I recall here an occasion of six years ago when I was asked to preach at a little gathering one Sunday evening about thirty miles from my home. This was a new congregation consisting mainly of one family. There were the grandparents, parents, and grandchildren. All together there were about a dozen folk present. These had all recently defected from the local Methodist church as they had felt led of the Lord.

It was a strange arrangement. The meeting house was no more than a large oblong wooden hut. There was a platform, a piano and a good number of seats, the majority of which were unoccupied.

As far as I was concerned I was just looking to the Lord for whatever He would have me to minister to these hungry hearted people.

The meeting commenced with singing and prayers led by the Pastor, until it was my time to speak.

As I felt the precious anointing of the Lord upon me, and often referring to the benefits of the baptism in the Holy Spirit, I urged that it was necessary for all of us to be enjoying His fullness.

As far as I was able to discern there was a completely negative response, even though the church had taken the name of Pentecostal — I expected someone to say "Praise the Lord" or "Amen" as is usual in these churches. Nevertheless, the folk were very gracious and kind, even to the extent of asking me to accept another invitation to preach there. Obviously my words did not fall on deaf ears, for some time later, a matter of two or three years, the leader of that group of Christians opened up his life to the Lord and received that inestimable blessing.

Since then the whole company has been transformed. God working mightily among them, one after another followed the leader as the hunger for the fullness of the Holy Spirit burned within them.

Today that church is moving in life. Their number

has increased, and the majority of them are now Spirit-filled believers, a testimony unto their Lord.

If John was a Baptist so was Jesus, 'For John truly baptized with water; but ye shall be baptized with the Holy Ghost . . .' On the day of Pentecost each and every one of the disciples who waited for the promised Holy Spirit received Him in fullness. Their lives were instantly charged with dynamic power and influence 'from on high'. They were not just personally blessed, wonderful though that would have been. Instead of being cold hearted, cowardly and self-protecting, even to the extent of hiding away behind closed doors for fear of the Jews and the violence that was being perpetrated against them, they became bold, lion-hearted men with a mission. They now possessed as it were a mandate from heaven to turn the world not upside down, but the right side up.

These men of God did not have to tell people that they had received the fullness of the Holy Spirit. It was so obvious for they were fearlessly doing the same works that Jesus did. They were changed, their words were penetrating, effectual, life-giving, comforting, healing, consoling, and whenever they spoke people listened.

Acts 2 is a very fascinating chapter. Here we see Peter who had earlier denied his Lord and Master with cursing and swearing moving in a new dimension. Now publicly identifying himself with Jesus, the lowly man of Calvary, Peter spoke with Holy Spirit vigour and passion. Standing up with his eleven colleagues, he lifted up his voice and addressed both the men of Judea and Jerusalem in defence of the risen Lord.

Peter told them who Jesus was. He also told them the purpose for which He came into the world, and why

He was so wickedly crucified by their evil hands. This man's newly received power and authority was tremendous. He even commanded the people to listen attentively to him, and they obeyed. "Men of Israel," said he, "Hear these words; Jesus of Nazareth, a man approved of God among you by miracles and wonders and signs, which God did by Him in the midst of you, as ye yourselves also know: Him, being delivered by the determinate council and foreknowledge of God, ye have taken, and by wicked hands have crucified and slain " (Acts 2:22,23).

Fervently he went on to tell them that God had indeed raised up that same Jesus from the dead, and that the Pentecostal power which was in evidence was nothing more or less than what God had long ago promised through His prophet Joel. "This is that," said Peter.

No one before this particular preacher had ever spoken like this. His authority was irresistible. He spoke with resignation, courage, love, and conviction, with power and a burning passion, yet with undeniable compassion.

After that type of preaching anyone would expect some response from the congregation. The Bible says 'they were pricked in their heart'. Convicted by the Holy Spirit, they did not know what to do with themselves. This was their open confession. The point was that they had now heard the truth. 'The Spirit of truth,' as Jesus called Him, was in control. These people had to face up to the facts as they really were. Their unjust hate of the Son of God became a terrifying burden such as they could no longer bear. Acknowledging their tremendous need, confessing their sin, and receiving forgiveness from the risen

Saviour was the only solution.

"Men and brethren" said they to the apostles, "what shall we do?" It is interesting to note here that this inquiry was not the result of a philosophic dissertation, nor was it the result of an argument. We cannot win souls to Christ through either of these means. It takes the presence and power of the Holy Spirit to lift up the Lord who alone has the prerogative to draw all men unto Himself.

Peter answered his questioners "Repent, and be baptized everyone of you in the name of Jesus Christ for the remission of sins, and ye shall receive the gift of the Holy Ghost." The Scriptures record that they gladly received this exhortation and were baptized. By the end of the day about three thousand of them were converted to Jesus Christ.

Was not that marvellous, considering that neither Peter nor any of his colleagues had ever been to Bible College? They had not had the time to fit it all in even if they were that way inclined. What Peter said was entirely without premeditation. He spoke as the Spirit prompted him, presenting the Word of life. I am old fashioned enough to believe that God requires, and expects no less from us today for fulfilling His will for our generation. "He that saith he abideth in Him (Jesus) ought himself also so to walk, even as He walked " (1 John 2:6).

CHAPTER TWO

GIVING

A genuine spiritual walk will never produce a mean character. Selfishness and the Holy Spirit cannot co-exist.

Our coming under the adjusting presence and power of the Spirit can be revolutionary. Our sense of values is bound to change. It was something like this that Jesus was illustrating to the rich young man who came to Him asking what he should do to inherit eternal life. He went away feeling very sorrowful when Jesus told him, "Sell all that thou hast, and distribute unto the poor, and thou shalt have treasure in heaven: and come, follow me " (Luke 18:22).

Obviously Jesus was not setting out to destroy this fellow. That was farthest from His thoughts. He didn't mean that he had to be destitute to be accepted into God's family. Jesus was pointing to a full life, a completeness in the LORD not bounded by earthly possessions.

There is such a thing as deceitful riches against which we are warned in the Bible (Matthew 13:22). This man was deceived. His life was controlled by the things he possessed. He was notoriously rich, but only in this world's goods. It is far better to gain notoriety for faith in the Lord than for being rich. "If riches increase," says the Psalmist David, "set not your heart upon them " (Psalm 62:10). Jesus warns us that it is really no profit at all for us to gain the whole world at the expense of our soul.

Actually life does not consist in riches. It is a matter of seeking 'first the Kingdom of God and His righteousness' and all that we need — and much more — will be added to us. I say much more, believing that our God is essentially very liberal. He does not only provide for our needs.

Many of us could live on a lot less than we do, we could live really frugally. If we had to we could exist on bread and water. We could manage with fewer changes of clothes, we could live in much cheaper dwellings. But what advertisement would that be for the Kingdom of God?

Our Heavenly Father desires immeasurably better than that for us. According to Deuteronomy Chapter 28 He has promised that His blessings will overtake us, and that He will bless our storehouses. We don't need storehouses if we are poverty stricken. If I had my way every preacher or teacher who is heard recommending poverty as God's will for His people would be 'struck off the list'.

The point is that walking in the Spirit involves our being more concerned with giving than getting. God will look after our getting. The life of Jesus portrayed this principle.

The Bible says 'For ye know the grace of our Lord Jesus Christ, that, though He was rich, yet for your sakes He became poor, that ye through His poverty might be rich' (2 Cor. 8:9). We might not have money to give to this one and that, but if we have it we should give it, lest the shame be on us rather than on the one in need. It is amazing how much God treasures this. He loves the cheerful giver, and delights to increase his substance.

For example Charlie Page was a poor young man when he cheerfully gave his first ten cents to God's work. That small sum was probably Charlie's first real investment in life. It involved self-denial. It demanded sacrifice, and a disciplined course of action contrary to his overwhelming personal demands and commitments. He had purposefully given those ten cents out of only one hundred, his entire wealth. It was God who had provided this amount of money for Charlie through the generosity of a Spirit-filled young lady who had discerned the need. And it was remarkable that at the time of handing him that dollar bill she also gave him something that was to be of eternal value. She gave him certain advice that was to change the whole course of his life.

She said something like this, "Give a tenth to God; make this your tithe. Practice tithing, give, give, go on giving, and you will never want again."

The young lady's advice impressed Charlie as much as did the dollar bill. As she spoke from God, she was giving expression to the very nature of God. How often we read in the Scriptures that 'God gave . . .' He so loved us 'that He gave His only begotten Son, that whosoever believeth in Him should not perish, but have everlasting life' (John 3:16).

As soon as Charlie found himself a job and was earning he began tithing regularly. Eventually he was not giving (investing) a tenth only, but much more, even as much as for the building of hospitals and other institutions for the benefit of his fellow men. He had prospered in heart and material things, as his heart encompassed the needs of others, and it should not be surprising when we are told that he became a millionaire and human benefactor.

The Church today is guilty of a grave blunder. She is neither portraying the excellence of life nor walking in the Spirit. Many of her money raising programmes are certainly open to question in the light of scriptural teaching. Once we get our principles right the way to prosperity in every realm is clear.

Paul says "Every man according as he purposeth in his heart, so let him give; not grudgingly, or of necessity: for God loveth a cheerful giver " (2 Cor. 9:7). He always blesses that principle which is of Himself. What about passing on some blessing from God's Word, some little gem perhaps that we may have gleaned, a word of comfort, consolation or cheer? God is seeking a people who willingly give back to Him, indeed who 'Worship Him in Spirit and in Truth'. We cannot understand these things with the unrenewed mind (see Romans 12:2). We certainly cannot find the Truth with our natural understanding. We find it by the Spirit. He leads us into the Truth.

If there was any other way that would be fine. Some folk might say that would be worth attempting, for we would then have reason for saying we have achieved something. But this will never be so. We are, so to speak, on a one way street where God has no other plans for us, but that we should be led by the Holy Spirit. This means that each of us must personally come into contact with Him. He makes Jesus Christ a constant living reality, so much so that we can confidently be fulfilling the will of God at all times. Romans 8:14 beautifully confirms this. 'For as many as are led by the Spirit of God, they are the sons of God'.

Surely He would never lead us to do anything that is not our Heavenly Father's will? 'He leads us in the paths of righteousness for His name's sake' giving, giving all the way. 'And we know that all things work together for good to them that love God, to them who are the called according to His purpose' (Romans 8:28).

In some respects who could have appeared more foolish than George Cutting as he cycled about the country preaching the Gospel. There seemed to be no real point in what he was doing.

He was no young man at this particular time, but having caught a vision from God in regard of the desperate needs of people everywhere on their way to a lost eternity, he trudged the countryside giving, giving life to everyone who would receive it. He was known to preach even where there was no one in sight. Foolish! Some of us might think so. But we cannot honestly think this when we remember that this man was being led by the Spirit of God. To prove the truth of this I shall here recount something miraculous that resulted from one such preaching.

He was in a lonely country place where as far as he could see there were very few houses around, just one here and there perhaps. Neither was there anyone in sight as he cycled along. Nevertheless, he felt like praising the Lord, and did, shouting as loud as he could, "Behold the Lamb of God, which taketh away the sin of the world." This he repeated twice only in fairly quick succession and went on his way. God was in this.

Some time later Mr Cutting was passing through the same place again and decided to diligently seek out every house and call at each door presenting the

Gospel. At one of the doors a little grey-haired woman of mature years, about five feet tall, faced him. He had hardly said hello before recognizing the life of Christ in her. She was radiant with the joy of the Lord and talking with the preacher about their mutual Saviour. Then asked Mr Cutting "When were you converted Mrs . . .?"

Her eyes lit up, and beaming with delight she said, "About six months ago."

"Go on, tell me what happened" he continued.

"Well, it was like this" she explained. "I was inside here in a very distressed state. Knowing that I was a sinner in need of a Saviour, I was kneeling down making every effort to find Him. Crying unto God with all my heart, He heard me and shouted "Behold the Lamb of God which taketh away the sin of the world." I wasn't quite sure what He had said so I quickly asked Him to repeat it for me and He did. Straightaway I knew that I should repent of my sins. This I did and accepted Jesus into my life. Oh it was wonderful!"

Of course it was wonderful! God was moving by His Spirit, leading His servant George Cutting and maintaining the reality of Christ in him wherever he went so that he was able to be giving. This in fact is what a good many of us lack today, the vibrant life of Christ. Without His Spirit's moving we languish in powerlessness.

CHAPTER THREE

ONENESS

Why is there little or no spiritual life in so many churches today? Surely this is because the Holy Spirit is ignored. In some places He is not given an opportunity to do anything. Let us look at these more closely. They have their religious programmes. They are well organized. They are very sincere. But they do not realize that 'It is the Spirit that "giveth" life' and not the programme, not the organization, not any human effort. Unless the Holy Spirit is present working in, upon and through God's redeemed people, Christ is not uplifted. Consequently sinners are not brought into vital contact with God, such as the uplifting of Christ is always sure to do.

The Bible says 'Now we have received, not the Spirit of the world, but the Spirit which is of God; that we might know the things that are freely given to us of God' (1 Cor. 2:12). The Holy Spirit is God's free gift to the Church, to everyone who will receive Him.

There are many people today who are sick in their minds, sick in their bodies, so sick that some of them succumb to taking their own lives. Why? Because of the lack of the knowledge of God. They do not know that He has made provision for them and they do not know that this provision is in the present tense, a reality to be experienced *now* by the Holy Spirit.

Indeed we live in the 'now' and His Word is surely for now. God has not changed. He loves us all the time. This love has been challenged in every possible way. Jesus was the full expression of God's love, revealing as He did to us the love of the Father by healing, not making sick nor destroying. So He declares that He has not come like the thief (the Devil) to steal, to kill and to destroy, but has come to give life.

Jesus presents everybody with His message of salvation. He counters every challenge by the way He lived. Where people would continue to live in spiritual darkness He comes to give them His own Spirit so that they may have light and be light.

No one can just sit back and say Jesus' way is only a way of salvation. Surely His is the only way, the only solution to our present need, the means by which people of varying backgrounds can be united in a common purpose. When the truth of this begins to affect us other people will also be affected. I remember another friend of mine telling me about her visit to a ladies' meeting one afternoon. She began talking with the ladies about Jesus' Spirit being the river of water of life. She told her listeners that He had done so much for her in salvation, healing her own sick body, and converting so many souls through the ministry He had given her, that her life was now full of nothing but love for Him.

"He is here now" she declared. "He is here in all His resurrection power! Jesus is alive and He loves you! I have been changed and this could happen to you!"

For over an hour my friend told them truths about Jesus both from His Word and from personal experiences. Then a woman sitting at the back of the meeting tearfully raised her right arm exclaiming "I am healed!" Her arm which had for some time been paralysed from a stroke was now well, whole again. Others too, probably every one who was present received some precious touch from the Lord of Glory, for the life of God was flowing as a river from heaven through the speaker to the people.

Some of us are concerned as we see people getting together forming what they call the Ecumenical Movement. They see a great need for unity and feel they should do something about it. I believe as a substitute for God's ecumenity this Movement is doomed to failure. I cannot see anything in it that is right. Where is the Holy Spirit in the Movement? Where is the unifying bond? Does God call for unity of churches, of denominations or of the minds and hearts of His redeemed people?

There is only one foundation of unity and God has already established it. The apostle Paul acknowledged this and helps us considerably in 1 Cor. 3:11 by saying "For other foundation can no man lay than that is laid, which is Jesus Christ."

God has united us in His Son. No substitute for this unity will ever be suitable to God. So Jesus prayed in John 17 that we may be one even as He and the Father are one. We cannot be one in religion and theology, but we can be one in Jesus Christ.

We are exhorted too in Ephesians 4 to endeavour to 'Keep the unity of the Spirit'. This does not mean that we have to get together and devise some means or other of sinking our differences in a common pool. Oh no! God has already done for us in Christ all that is necessary, and we should constantly be hearing His 'still small voice' registering in our hearts the full appreciation of this. Words like these should always be in our minds, "Keep yourselves in the love of God. Stay in that in which I have put you."

God is always sure to work wherever His people are found united. This is a cardinal principle of His dealings with His children. He is bound to this condition by His own Word. "Behold, how good and how pleasant it is for brethren to dwell together in unity! It is like the precious ointment upon the head, that ran down upon the beard, even Aaron's beard: that went down to the skirts of his garment; as the dew of Hermon, and as the dew that descended upon the mountains of Zion: for there the Lord commanded the blessing, even life for evermore " (Psalm 133).

Here then is the principle of ecumenity devised in heaven without any human aid. Nothing can be added to this nor taken away.

David who composed this Psalm was thrilled as he saw God's wonderful plan for blessing His people with the Holy Spirit. So he exclaimed "Behold . . .!" In other words look and see for yourself how delightful it is for people to be living peaceably and in harmony with one another! The virtue in this 'togetherness' or oneness in purpose and relationship he would say, is as much of God as was Aaron's anointing oil. It was invaluable in the sense that it was prepared in accordance with God's specific instructions. All its ingredients were prescribed by God, and its application was also in accord with His command.

David would go on to say, note that the ointment did not even touch Aaron's flesh, for "the flesh profiteth nothing." But it ran down from his head onto his beard and all over his clothes which were also specially made to God's own specifications.

Finding a people who can be likened to this perfect anointing which is wholly pleasing to Himself, God cannot help pouring out His Holy Spirit upon them. They are in the right condition to accept His power, as they are enjoying His ecumenity. God is no dictator. He will never go against our free will, forcing Himself upon us, taking over our lives and dictating to us. If we do not want Him He will never compel us to accept Him. If we do not choose to accept His ecumenity He will never force us. Force is not a part of the Holy Spirit's work. He is gentle, so beautifully gentle that we can even quench and grieve Him. Truly He is a 'gentle man'.

It is important for us to understand clearly that the Holy Spirit has not come to give us unity. We already have this in Christ, and the Holy Spirit will help us to maintain it if we let Him. Have we any idea of how He does this?

In John 15 we read of Jesus promising that when the Spirit of Truth comes He will exalt Him (Jesus), indeed bringing us into all the truth that He taught. It is obvious then that He only speaks of Jesus, bringing to our hearts and minds lovely things about Him. He points one way only, to our Redeemer.

The Holy Spirit is always free to come upon the individual Christian who looks to the Lord for such a supernatural visitation. The question that immediately arises in the minds of some of us is this. Why then do so many people struggle and strive to no avail, if all we have to do is ask?

CHAPTER FOUR

RECEIVING THE BAPTISM

Often the greatest hindrance to receiving the baptism in the Spirit is in the striving and struggling. This approach is not recommended in the Bible, and we are not likely to receive anything from God by this method.

Listen to what Jesus says about receiving the Spirit. "If you then, being evil, know how to give good gifts unto your children: how much more shall your Heavenly Father give the Holy Spirit to them that ask Him?" (Luke 11:13). Since the day of Pentecost nearly two thousand years ago there has not been the need for waiting or tarrying for the Spirit. The out-pouring continues to this day, and it only remains for us to appropriate that which is already made available. It is amazing though, how some people would miss God's best by making this matter of receiving complicated!

Many who fail to be able to receive are folk who say that they have very much faith. This is absurd! They confess belief in God's Word, and appear to be very sincere and genuine in their desires. This is strange, but not quite so strange when we remember that real faith is a possessor. It never talks about itself, but acts out its presence by doing and receiving. James 1:22 says "be ye doers of the Word, and not hearers only, deceiving your own selves."

Faith is like the leaven in a lump of dough. It is a living and active force quite unobtrusively working to accomplish its aims. So for the Christian desiring to be baptized in the Spirit it is essential not to pretend or imagine being in possession of any spiritual virtue beforehand. It is sufficient for us to simply come to God, making our particular request known. He already knows our hearts.

That woman of whom we read in Mark 5 who had been sick for 12 years is a good example of one who has faith. She came to Jesus just as she was. To her that haemorrhage was a tremendous mountain that could only be removed by Someone greater than all she had so far seen.

She had sought help from all the best doctors in town. Suffering much at their hands, she had paid out all the money she had on their fees. She had taken the medicines they had given her, and she was still sick, and not only that, she was getting worse.

When she heard of Jesus, however, and perceived in her heart that He had the solution to her trouble, then, moved by faith she immediately decided to do something. Nothing could stop her from getting to Him, not even the great crowd and possible commotion. Her faith heightening, she concluded that if only she could get near enough to touch even His clothes she would be healed.

Making her way through the crowd, her heart pounding, at last she was within reach of Jesus. Being so near to the Lord was tremendous. But that was not enough. She had to actively stretch out her arm. This was the moment for which she had longed, the very climax of her decision.

Now she touched the Life Giver, and what happened? Verse 29 says 'straightway the fountain of her blood was dried up; and she felt in her body that she was healed of that plague'.

What was Jesus' reaction to this? He too felt something. The Bible tells us that He knew that virtue had gone out of Him, and confirming the miraculous healing that had taken place in the woman, He said, "Daughter, thy faith hath made thee whole . . . ."

It is particularly interesting to note that this woman did not hope that if she touched the Lord's clothes she would be healed. She already knew that she would be, and was carrying this knowledge in her heart as a settled fact. The Bible says 'now faith is the substance of things hoped for, the evidence of things not seen,' (Heb. 11:1). Here we have to distinguish between faith and hope.

Hope enabled her to start on the faith journey to Jesus. This was basically very good, but not enough to entirely meet her needs. There were quite possibly many others equally sick and clamouring around Jesus, but without any faith. Consequently they had nothing with which to draw the virtue from the Saviour. What was enough for her though in her particular need was that her heart possessed the evidence of her healing, the very end product of her implicit faith which was initiated by that 'hope (which) maketh not ashamed'. In coming to the Lord for the baptism in the Spirit this same principle applies.

We do not come to Him hoping to be baptized. We already know that we will be, as surely as we know that He says he that asks receives. My feeling is that many Christians are not really satisfied in doing only this. They pray and pray and keep on praying without doing any receiving. They do not understand that God cannot do the receiving for them. Typical of this type of person is this woman whose situation I shall describe.

She was middle aged and a firm lover of the Lord Jesus. The first time I ever met her was at a little Mission Hall where I had been preaching and she asked me to pray for her. I like praying for people, so I replied "Certainly! What do you want God to do for you?"

"Pray that I may receive the baptism in the Spirit, please" she said.

"Have you ever had prayer for this before?" I inquired.

"Oh yes, several times over the years and I pray myself every day, but I've never received" she said with firm resignation as though she already knew that she would not get that for which she was asking. Despite her doubts she would have prayer as usual.

Pausing for a second or two, I waited upon the Lord as to what I should do. He was certainly in this matter, and I was immediately fired with the right questions and answers. "Why haven't you so far received?" I asked her.

"I don't know!" she replied smiling.

"Would you like to receive at this very moment?"

"Yes, please" she assured me.

"Well" I continued "all you have to do now is to receive (accept) by faith when I pray. Whether you feel that you have received anything or not, believe that you have. Then thank God for His wonderful gift, and start praising Him."

Agreeing with me she soon bowed her head and I began to pray. When I stopped she thanked God for the oncoming of His Spirit. Speaking with Him in tones which reflected a real sense of personal relationship with the Lord, her life was manifestly changed. She had all this time been like a flower in bud, but now at last she had come into bloom. Filled with the Holy Spirit of Truth, she was talking with her heavenly Father in a new tongue, a language which she had never learned. Marvellous!

Asking the Lord once only for this precious gift is certainly enough, so long as we truly believe that we receive — see Mark 11:24 and 1 John 5:14,15.

CHAPTER FIVE

NOT BY MIGHT

Jesus did not really reveal Himself, did not really 'bloom' and show His true identity as God's witness until the Holy Spirit had descended upon Him at His water baptism at the river Jordan (Matt. 3:16).

From that time He began to show and declare who He really was. This was the beginning of His life of signs and wonders. People were astonished at the words that came out of His mouth. They were spirit and they were life. Some said "Never man spake like this man." He turned water into wine, cleansed lepers, raised the dead, cast out demons and healed many that were sick. Wherever He went people benefited from His presence. It is recorded in Luke 4:18 that He said "The Spirit of the Lord is upon Me, because He hath anointed Me to . . ." Note that He did not say of Himself He was going to do anything. He declared Himself as being under the authority of the Holy Spirit.

The way of the Spirit to those who move in Him is truly wonderful. 'For it is God which worketh in you both to will and to do of His good pleasure' (Phil. 2:13), just as it was with Jesus.

What was Jesus going to do? In the words of Scripture, 'Preach the Gospel to the poor; heal the

brokenhearted, preach deliverance to the captives . . . '
restore people to normal conditions. Here He was
testifying that in His weakness He could do nothing.
Yet by the Holy Spirit He did everything. This
certainly shows that humanly speaking He was as weak
and often tired as any of us, but now He was moving
not according to His own feelings, will, ability,
strength, or even desire, but by the power of the Holy
Spirit.

So we cannot say it was all right for Jesus, He could
not help doing everything right, and well, He had all
the power! No! On the contrary He was in Himself
helpless. He came to do what His Father told Him to
do, and only by the Spirit could He do it.

Can we say then that the Church can do anything
without the Holy Spirit? Of course not! God is revealing
Himself to the Church by His Spirit through Jesus. He
is the solution to everybody's need and must be
revealed. The Lord said something like this, "It is good
for Me to go away, you will benefit from this for the
Holy Spirit will then come and explain what I have
been saying to you. With His help you are also going to
understand My Father and Me much better. He is
going to lead you into all the Truth, and help you in
every way. Everything that you need, all that I was to
you, He will be. You will not have to consider what to
say in your own defence when you find yourself in
straits. The Holy Spirit shall give you what to say."

The time came when a Spirit-filled Christian was the
rule rather than the exception. So real was the
presence, power and authority of the Holy Spirit in the
early Church that new Christians were soon, if not
immediately upon conversion, filled and vitally caught
up in the spiritual life of the ever increasing Company.

Wherever these Christians found themselves they caused a revolution, a change in the lives of others. This was no more than their Lord had done before them.

The Scriptures declare that He was the Light of the World. By the Holy Spirit His life was so prolific in its yield of fruitfulness to God that God could not help opening up the heavens twice over, and publicly commending Jesus on each occasion as the Son of His delight, once at the river Jordan at His baptism, and again at the mount of transfiguration. Nothing like this had ever happened before in all the history of the world. Such was the result of a life lived in the Spirit continually in God's presence.

God never once failed Jesus. Neither will He fail us. Filled with the Holy Spirit our lives too are bound to be a delight to God. Stephen was full of the Holy Spirit. Consider him standing up in that ungodly crowd. He confounded the great men of his day. The Bible says 'They were not able to resist the wisdom and the Spirit by which he spake' (Acts 6:10). His words were invincible, full of Divine power against a villainous society.

Stephen's life was so pleasing to his Lord and Master that when he was martyred something peculiarly wonderful happened in heaven, something of which the Bible bears record but once only. Jesus of whom we read as seated at the right hand of God, 'stood up' welcoming His friend, Stephen, home to glory.

The text says 'He, (Stephen) being full of the Holy Ghost, looked up steadfastly into heaven, and saw the Glory of God, and Jesus "standing" on the right hand of God' (Acts 7:55).

I believe Jesus was so excited, so thrilled with the

finished work of the Holy Spirit in His friend that He could not restrain Himself from showing some emotion. In the words of the late W.F.P. Burton (founder of the Congo Evangelistic Mission) "They — the ungodly — can kill us on the job, but they cannot drive us from it, for the Word of God is still the power of God unto salvation." Stephen's experience certainly confirms Mr Burton's statement. His life was not taken from him. His enemies thought they had killed him on the job, but the Bible assures us that he 'fell asleep'. Isn't this what we all do after a hard day's work?

Completely sold out to the Lord, he had been very busy. Stephen had a tremendous job to do in a very short time. His brethren must have been amazed, and yet thrilled by all that he did. How fruitful was his life as God's love radiated through him, defying the forces of the Devil, rescuing, and bringing many people into contact with the risen Christ!

The brethren had chosen Stephen to be a church officer, laid their hands on Him and blessed him. No doubt they were looking forward to his good service in the Church administration. But no one can control the Holy Spirit. A man empowered by Him for doing exploits in Jesus' name cannot be tied down to any particular task. Wherever the Holy Spirit leads he follows. His sole ambition is to exalt Christ, and he is equipped for shedding His heavenly light everywhere.

With the presence and power of the Holy Spirit upon Stephen's life, he accomplished more for the Kingdom of God in one preaching than do many evangelical folk in a whole lifetime. God duly promoted him to Glory from the midst of a hostile world. It was not surprising that this man having been so much in tune with heaven, his closing words echoed the same sentiments as his Saviour's last words "LORD, lay not this sin to their charge." So it is not a matter of how intellectual we are when it comes to the things of God, but whether we are really filled with the Spirit.

We ought not to be trying to convince the world intellectually. We do not have to prove to people that we are human, they understand that; at least most of them do. No matter how clever we might be in our theology, and cultured in our forms of worship, we can be spiritually barren, a far cry from the life-style of our Spirit-filled first century predecessors. Being filled with the Spirit means we are ready for anything.

I remember some time ago I had a very unpleasant task to perform. Bible in hand I called on a woman who was living in immorality. Some seventy miles from her home and family, she was living with a man who was not her own husband.

Constrained by the Holy Spirit, I felt it my duty to go and advise her to repent of her sin, her adulterous life, and return home to her family. As soon as she saw me she was aware of the purpose of my visit, and asking me inside the bedsitter, she gave me a seat on a chair at the foot of the bed. In the 'natural' this was extremely dangerous. At any moment the man might appear. What might his reaction to my presence be?

It was, in a way, like being inside a lion's den with the lion lying down just outside the door. Should he chance to come into where I was sitting what could I do? — Run for my life? I sat a virtually defenceless prey.

Such considerations are human and natural. But I was not walking in either. My human reasoning had little or no part in this matter, as I sat speaking of my

Saviour's prescription for our way of living. My message began having its effect and she started expressing her feelings of guilt.

Suddenly I heard footsteps outside. They became louder and louder, then a pause. The next thing was that the door into the bedsitter was being slowly opened from the outside. In my heart I knew what was happening, I knew that the man had arrived, but I kept looking into my open Bible which I held in my left hand, and often glancing up at the woman sitting opposite me. The door opened wide, I looked in that direction to see the man standing there.

He was nearly twice my size, a giant of a man. Facing me squarely he glowered at me like a huge cat waiting to pounce on its prey. I was not in the least afraid. The confidence and poise that the Holy Spirit maintained in me at that moment was tremendous. It burned within my breast, as I looked the man in the eye and said in very firm tones "go away, I am on the Lord's business."

There is no difficulty in imagining what followed. Turning on his heels the man walked away as quiet as a lamb, and as long as I was there never returned. Not only was his mouth stopped, but his hands were stayed. "Not by might, nor by power, but by My Spirit, saith the Lord of Hosts."

CHAPTER SIX

BAPTISM

The baptism in the Spirit is really the door into all that we have so far been discussing. What do we mean by 'baptism?' Why not be satisfied with some other terminology such as fullness of the Spirit, oncoming of the Spirit, Spirit-filled, filled with the Spirit, life in the Spirit . . .?

These are more expressive of a state of being, whereas 'baptism' relates to an irrevocable event. Firstly, the word baptism is Scriptural and aptly descriptive of immersion, appearing several times in the New Testament. Jesus asked a question, "The baptism of John, was it from heaven, or of men?" John, of course, was baptizing in water only. That type of baptism has its own particular significance, as the Scriptures distinctly show us, for everybody who has repented of his sins and turned to God through faith in Jesus Christ. Romans 6 speaks of water baptism as signifying death, burial and resurrection with Christ who Himself said, "Suffer it to be so now: for thus it becometh us to fulfill all righteousness" (Matt. 3:15).

While John was baptizing the converts he had won for the Kingdom of heaven, he told them of another type of baptism which would necessitate someone mightier than himself to perform. "He that sent me" said John "to baptize with water, the same said unto me, upon whom thou shalt see the Spirit descending, and remaining on Him, the same is He (Jesus) which baptizeth with the Holy Ghost" (John 1:33).

It was not long after John had said this that his words were fulfilled, for Jesus came to him desiring to be baptized. John did baptize Him, and it was immediately afterwards that according to Luke 3:22 "The Holy Ghost descended in a bodily shape like a dove upon Him . . . ."

Jesus' receiving the Holy Spirit in this particular way was very significant. He was now equipped of God with the ability to minister in a new dimension, and that as the head of the Church He (Jesus) would eventually baptize His followers in the same Spirit.

Has Jesus accomplished this work? The Day of Pentecost marks the beginning of the great outpouring. He launched His Church in the blaze of the Holy Spirit. What Christ had received of His Father He would share with His loved ones.

It is important to note that the unregenerate cannot receive the baptism in the Holy Spirit. This is only for born again people. Jesus speaks of this in John 14:17, "Even the Spirit of truth; whom the world cannot receive . . . ." This is reserved for us who have been redeemed "Not of corruptible seed, but of incorruptible, by the Word of God" (1 Peter 1:23).

The baptism in the Spirit is not a goal in itself. It is the gateway to a goal. It is the means by which we arrive at an enlarged or greater appreciation of Jesus. We are baptized (immersed) in the Spirit that we may live in that realm seven days a week, three hundred and sixty five days a year, every minute of every day in the Spirit, until Jesus returns, and even then we shall remain in the Spirit. I believe this to be so 'but as it is written, eye hath not seen, nor ear heard, neither have entered into the heart of man, the things which God hath prepared for them that love Him. But God hath revealed them unto us by His Spirit: for the Spirit searcheth all things, yea, the deep things of God' (1 Cor. 2:9,10).

We can know the Bible thoroughly — every verse, from cover to cover; go to Bible school; regularly attend church; and yet know nothing of this spiritual life. Peter and John were 'unlearned and ignorant men,' but filled with the Holy Spirit they were mighty through God. They were well known in heaven for their obedience to their Master, well known on earth for their revolutionary preaching, and well known in hell for their dexterity in the use of the sword of the Spirit. These men knew both how to do and to endure.

Talking about endurance, Paul the apostle, was no mean example. He was a man of immense spiritual stature. His response to adversity is very revealing. Sustained by the Spirit, Paul could always see beyond the sufferings of this life. In Philippians 3 he says "I count all things but loss for the excellency of the knowledge of Christ Jesus my Lord . . . ." It is evident that this man's only goal in life was Christ.

If some of us should find ourselves being buffetted about like Paul was, what would our reactions be? Perhaps none of us can really give an answer at this stage. But these were some of the many sufferings through which he passed. He was shipwrecked, beaten with rods; stoned and left for dead in the street at Lystra.

It is so easy in such circumstances, isn't it, to ask why

should this happen to me? What have I done to deserve this? But in the face of it all listen to Paul's declaration. "For our light affliction, which is but for a moment, worketh for us a far more exceeding and eternal weight of glory; while we look not at the things which are seen, but at the things which are not seen: for the things that are seen are temporal; but the things which are not seen are eternal" (2 Cor. 4:17,18).

Many who claim to be baptized in the Holy Spirit stop short here, and are not good adverts for life in the Spirit. In times of crises they fail to be able to courageously endure hardship. What is the real reason behind this?

Here we need to understand something more about the difference between the baptism in the Spirit and walking in the Spirit. The former ushers us into a brand new way of life and the latter is concerned with our behaviour in that new way. This is not a fluctuating existence. It is not a life of praising the Lord in church and grumbling at home. It is not a life of joy when we are in the company of fellow Christians, and doubts and fears when we are on our own facing trials and temptations.

The believer who is Holy-Spirit-constrained is consistent and trustworthy. He possesses that calm, that tranquility which is characteristic of folk who are enjoying the 'rest' of God. As it says in Hebrews 4 'there remaineth therefore a rest to the people of God'. Why should they be robbed of this? 'For he that is entered into his rest, he also hath ceased from his own works, as God did from His' (Heb. 4:9,10). The Bible also declares 'walk in the Spirit, and ye shall not fulfil the lust of the flesh' (Gal. 5:16).

However, we must never be unsympathetic toward

folk whose life and walk in the Spirit fluctuate. May God grant us continually hearts that are tender in regard of our brothers and sisters who will be helped. Rather than ridicule, what they really need is encouragement in the Lord who is the God of all grace. From time to time all of us appreciate, and in fact need, a little help and encouragement. We need to help one another to develop spiritually, and continue drinking unceasingly from 'the fountain of living waters'.

In this relation Jeremiah 2:13 is very helpful, 'For my people have committed two evils; they have forsaken me the fountain of living waters, and hewed them out cisterns, broken cisterns, that can hold no water.' What does this mean?

In the context that we are speaking it means that some of us have failed to 'endure hardness, as a good soldier of Jesus Christ' (2 Tim. 2:3). We have ceased being resourceful and effective because we are not drawing upon His bountiful supply. I believe anything that is allowed to come between us and our reading and meditating in the Word of God can be a 'broken cistern'. Nowadays there are some Christians who are claiming that they do not need to read the Bible. How absurd! The more advanced we become in the things of God the greater our need is of spiritual food, the Word of God which is 'able to make thee wise unto salvation through faith which is in Christ Jesus.' It is the only thing that can help us through life's journey, maintaining us in spiritual vigour.

CHAPTER SEVEN

EFFECTIVENESS

What is the opposite to spiritual vigour? The Bible speaks of the soul and the spirit. In the soul realm we can only know things that we have learned, things that we memorize. Spiritual vigour does not depend on what we know. It depends on the operation of the Holy Spirit upon the Word of God in our lives.

Hebrews Chapter 4 is remarkably helpful here 'For the Word of God is quick, and powerful . . . .' It is not weak and subject to alteration. It cannot be bent to suit our particular circumstances. It is the most powerful thing in the whole world, and can divide between soul and spirit. There can be much more activity in the soul realm than in the spirit. To the unsuspecting this can be very deceptive. But anybody who comes to God and lets Him apply His Word to his life will inevitably experience a tremendous change.

Just speaking a few words in tongues, on its own, is not an evidence that the speaker is under the constraint of the Holy Spirit. If we are going to have a real Holy Spirit manifestation in our lives something far more than the ability to speak in tongues has to take place in us. God's Word must begin to have such sway in our lives that we become effective not only in word but in deed.

It is for this very purpose that He is pouring His Spirit upon us, that through the operation of the Holy Spirit we might be the solution to many a desperate need in the world. 'For we know that the whole creation groaneth and travaileth in pain together until now . . . for the manifestation of the sons of God.' And who are these sons? They are the people with Holy Ghost power and ability such as was seen in the Church in the early days after Pentecost displaying the life of Christ.

There is one great doorway through which each of us and the whole Church must become effective. Faith is that doorway. Only through faith can a child of God be competent in His service. We might possess many wonderful talents and abilities. We might have wisdom that is able to operate without the help of the Holy Spirit and be able to confound many people.

The early Church suffered from men with great talents of speech, of wisdom, of persuasion, and Paul spoke about these clever people, who are able to dissuade folk from the original truth, as it is in Jesus, into error. But if we are going to be effective to the tearing down of strongholds and establishing something that is of eternal value, it will only be done as the revelation of faith dawns upon our souls.

What was it that was singularly noteworthy about the apostles? They were all filled with the Holy Spirit and whatever they said or did was by the Spirit and was effectual.

Filled with the Holy Spirit we do not have to ask God for power, we simply have to use it. We only know how much we have by using it. The widow and the cruse of oil mentioned in 1 Kings 17 is a good example of effectiveness. She could see that she had so much oil,

but as far as she could tell it was not enough to meet
the needs of the people who were present. By faith,
however, not just blind faith, but faith in God, she
started to pour out from what she had. What was the
result? As she poured, God poured. The little amount
that she had thought was not enough, was ample as
long as she continued pouring. Her little was
connected to God's plenty.

When we have experienced only a little of God's
power in our lives, and begin to use that little we are
immediately connected to the very source, the 'All
Power' of which Jesus spoke as having been given into
His hand. He is our Head, and we understand from
Ephesians 1 that this same power is working in us. But
it has to be released. How? Through faith.

The Lord talked about the tongue. The tongue is
one of the greatest hindrances to faith. The power of
life and death is in the tongue. Before we can know a
Holy Spirit ministry of faith and become effective in
the Church of God, we must allow the Holy Spirit to
first take control of our tongue. It must no longer move
at the dictates of the mind, but at the promptings of
the Spirit. The Lord does not dwell in the mind. He
does not completely make new the mind even at the
new birth, nor at the baptism in the Holy Spirit. God
dwells in the heart, and it is from here that the Spirit's
promptings come. It is a principle of Divine order that
we bring our minds into subjection to the Spirit.

Having at last found somebody in ourselves who is
more than conqueror we are going to challenge the
world. In ourselves we are weak, but on the other hand
we are 'strong in the power of His might,' like the
apostle Peter was, or like Paul, like Stephen, John
Wesley or D.L. Moody. We have discovered the 'Christ

of God' and there is nothing too hard for Him.

Thus constituted, our mouths begin to speak and our tongues begin to declare, not the wisdom of the mind, but what the Spirit says. He is saying something, and we are not dependent on any of the five natural senses to tell out what He is saying, but on faith that springs from our heart.

So there is nothing now to hinder our spiritual progress individually, nor is there anything to impede the Church unless we are looking in the natural for what is spiritual. With our five senses we are capable of arriving at almost everything. Consequently, it is easy for some of us to be deceived into waiting for something dramatic to — as it were — come over us to tell us that we are in the Spirit.

Yet we only have to glance again at what happened to the disciples. No sooner had they received the baptism in the Holy Spirit than they began to do something. The Bible says 'With great power gave the apostles witness of the resurrection of the Lord Jesus: and great grace was upon them all' (Acts 4:33). Being in the power of the Spirit — we are always active in our Father's business.

This is where effectiveness comes into its own. It can be measured by our portrayal of God's benevolence in the world, and how many people we bring to belief and faith in His saving grace. This is not to say that in ourselves we have the ability to effect salvation for anyone. Far be the thought, but the Holy Spirit's power that is at work in us is concerned with bringing the unregenerate to the saving knowledge of Christ.

Our part really is to be always available to the Holy Spirit. He will work through us for the advancement of the testimony of the One whom He is here to glorify. In this connection no limit is put on us. We are constituted witnesses. Who can measure the degree or quality of our witness?

Jesus said "I, if I be lifted up from the earth, will draw all men unto me." When a person receives Christ as Saviour he has the basic essentials for a lifetime of exploration and adventure such as he had never thought possible. He is endowed with a brand new concept of living. There is something about him that can be acknowledged as Christ-centredness.

For this brand new life to be sustained in freshness and effective witnessing, it must of necessity be endued with like power. When we speak of business some unsuspecting folk might have difficulty in distinguishing between the many social activities inside and outside the Church, and what the Holy Spirit is doing. The contrast is clear. None of us has any right to criticize social work. Rather, we could often do something more than we are already doing in support of it. But the fact remains that being on our Father's business will always be demonstrated by the extent to which God uses us with manifest results.

Unless we are demonstrating the presence of the Lord in the world it is anybody's right to question whether we are really effective.

It can hardly be overstressed that we do not within ourselves contain the solution to the world's problems. Jesus never taught that we should even attempt trying to solve them. Nowhere in Scripture are we taught that we should. Nevertheless, we do not dismiss them as though they were not there. The Holy Spirit in our individual lives makes us an invaluable part of the solution instead of a continual part of the problem.

In our witness unto the One we represent He enables

us to effectively lead many a wounded sin-crushed soul out of the turmoil into glorious liberty in Christ.

Success and effectiveness are not one and the same. We might be tremendously successful in material things and hopelessly lacking in effectiveness. This will be especially so if in what we have amassed, whether money or this world's goods, there is no public expression of gratitude to God. There is a sense in which all that we may ever presume to possess at any given time belongs to Him anyway. If the success then is held as a sign of approval from God, and a means to demonstrate His benevolent nature, that is fine; that is the work of the Lord.

We have only to study the lives of Abraham, Hezekiah and Solomon, to name but a few great tycoons of the past, to see that success can be wholly related to God. But there can be, and often is, danger in this realm. Remember Jesus saying that it is easier for a camel to go through the eye of a needle than for a rich man to enter heaven. The trouble starts with us when riches increase. The need for dependence on God consequently decreases and becomes the harbinger of spiritual decline. Sad to say this happens all too often, but there is good news from heaven today. 'Give, and it shall be given unto you; good measure, pressed down, and shaken together, and running over, shall men give into your bosom. For with the same measure that ye mete withal it shall be measured to you again' (Luke 6:38).

It is doubtful whether there can be a safer way of acquiring all that we shall ever need. The revealed presence of the Giver of the Word is guaranteed by the Holy Spirit. He is the precious Effector of all that God has promised.

Do not forget Jesus demonstrated the presence of His Father God by performing signs and wonders. Where was His commitment? Not to culture, not to success, to society, social services, but to God. What Jesus did was effectiveness, *par excèllence*, and this should be our aim, to be about our Father's business.

CHAPTER EIGHT

FAITH IN ACTION

God has already told us in His Word exactly where He has put us. He has put us in Christ. This is the most exalted position there can be, and from here by the Holy Spirit we can move from one degree of faith to another.

It is a Divine principle that everything that God has given us can only be appropriated by faith. Also, the expression of everything that He has given us by promise is limited to our willingness. God can never make us more effective than we are prepared to let Him do through our faith. I once had an experience which though not wholly applicable to the present matter illustrates this principle. While I was in Copenhagen a few years ago, preaching the Gospel in the open air one evening with a local group of Christians, the enemy struck at our party.

But for the grace of God we might have all scampered away like scared rabbits. Where we had gathered in what became known to me as the Walking Street, there were also many drunkards, some of whom were aimlessly staggering around, while others were sitting on benches and not seeming to care much about anything. One of my Danish colleagues was standing in front of a portable microphone preaching, when out of the large crowd of listening folk a man in a half-drunken state came staggering up to him.

This man had a tray in his hands on which were two glasses of beer — or some other alcoholic beverage. He held out the tray to the preacher offering him a drink. Unperturbed, the preacher declined the offer and continued addressing the gathering. The man became very indignant, drank both glasses of the beverage and hurried away with the tray and the empty glasses. I presume he took them back to the place from which he acquired the drinks. Now, more greatly under the influence of alcohol than at first, with fists clenched, he returned like a ferocious bull thundering his way up to the preacher.

He rested his hand on the preacher's left shoulder, and was just about to strike him with his right fist when a man intervened. Minor skirmishes among the other drunks immediately ensued, and it appeared as though the whole occasion would end in disarray.

There was a disturbing simulated scuffle between the preacher's assailant and defender. The former retained his hold on the preacher's shoulder. Without offering any resistance or defence, the preacher continued proclaiming his message. This was stupendous. The Holy Spirit was in control of the entire situation. The Christians, numbering about thirty or forty quickly huddled together close to the preacher and with one accord asked God to save this disturber of the peace. We prayed that the love of Jesus might overwhelm him.

Our faith was evidently released unto God, and in front of, I suppose, about a thousand folk, a miracle that I shall never forget took place. We witnessed no angelic intervention. There was no thunder, no smoke or lightning, no cloud, just a profusion of tears.

That disturber was now a broken man. Having become sober within an instant, he cried unto the Lord for mercy. "I am sorry, I am sorry, I am sorry . . ." he repeated. By the end of the evening's meeting, soundly converted, he was one with us testifying to the grace of God. Next evening the same man dressed in probably his best clothes was among the first of the Christians on the site giving out Tracts and witnessing for Jesus, chiefly among the drunks, his late companions.

Faith in God does move the mighty mountain. Faith in God does calm the troubled sea. We can only be effective in our ministry to people, whether they be drunkards or not, according to the degree of faith we will allow the Lord to release within us. He wants to bless us much more than we have already been blessed, loving us and loving many others into His Kingdom through us. In other words, with our little drop of oil, as we begin to love with this — even if we run out of love, perhaps for some unlovely person, God still loves him and so do we.

Today we almost take it for granted that 'the just shall live by faith'. But this did not easily become the foundation stone of our wonderful Christian heritage. We may recall with gratitude to God that this is what the Reformation was all about. Martin Luther after tremendous struggles with himself, his own intellect and those of others, received this treasured revelation from God; an amazing, indispensable rediscovery of the very centrality of the Christian belief and assurance which had been lost to the Church for centuries.

Finding that the rigours of penance and fasting, even to the point of death, did not help in possessing peace with his Maker, Martin Luther was soon to realize that the Holy Spirit had engendered liberty in his heart to make such an enduring stand for faith that would satisfy all tests.

With all the tradition, theology, dogma and superstition that abounded, how else could he have broken free? And what a price he paid; the scorn, the derision, the rejection which he was made to endure at the hands of the unspiritual and natural man, was grave.

Is it not amazing that the moment the fire of God begins to manifest itself in the life of any of us, others are sure to come along with their fire extinguishers trying desperately to dampen or put out that Divine glow. Real faith in God, however, will not relent. The Holy Spirit is behind it. He gives us the ability to believe God while others do not. Look at Abraham and the faith he had. It was not natural. 'Being not weak in faith' says Romans 4:19, 'he considered not his own body now dead, when he was about an hundred years old, neither yet the deadness of Sara's womb: he staggered not at the promise of God through unbelief; but was strong in faith, giving glory to God; and being fully persuaded that, what He had promised, He was able also to perform'.

The question arises as to how much faith does one need? The amount does not matter. What matters most is the quality as we have just seen in Abraham — his was strong.

To cite another, there was the Centurion of Matthew 8:5-13. He pleaded with Jesus, "Speak the word only, and my servant shall be healed." Jesus replied "I have not found so great faith, no, not in Israel." Also there was the woman of Matthew 15:22-28 who confidently asked Jesus to heal her daughter. How enthusiastically He answered her! "O woman, great is thy faith . . . ." Right through the Bible we find this quality of faith having power with God.

As Jesus taught His disciples to pray, He particularly stressed "Therefore I say unto you, what things soever ye desire, when ye pray, believe that ye receive them, and ye shall have them" (Mark 11:24).

The Bible is reputed to contain about thirty-three thousand promises made by God to His people who have faith. Many of us, however, are claiming these promises to no effect. Might it not be that on our part there is something missing, something subtly undermining our receiving that which is on offer from heaven? Let us not fail to recall the golden pathway that Jesus has shown that leads to everything we may need. He said "Seek ye first the Kingdom of God, and His righteousness; and all these things shall be added unto you" (Matt. 6:33).

It is easy to look around and try to copy other people's faith, only to find that the results are never the same as theirs. In any event we can neither work it up nor down.

Faith must come from God, Jesus being its Author and Finisher. Essentially then we must arrive at an end of ourselves. His presence must be all pervading for His faith to be manifested. The Adamic, fleshly nature must be fully surrendered unto God and superseded by the nature of Christ. Some of us to date are only concerned with yielding our conduct to the Lord. That is all well and good, but in the light of the Scriptural teaching of the new birth, this is surely not enough.

It has never been in the mind of God to make us better than we have been. Whether we are already

D

good natured or are the most vile, God requires that we must be new creations. Nothing of the nature of Adam must be carried over into the Christ-life. The more like Him we become the greater our faith shall be.

For myself, there has never been a time when I have felt satisfied that I have sufficient faith to please God. On the contrary, I am usually most distressed at heart at how ineffective I really am. This is particularly so after an apparently good rousing Holy Ghost time where I have been ministering, and where many have received their heart's desire. Some may have come to know Jesus Christ as personal Saviour; others may have received the baptism in the Holy Spirit, and still others been healed, delivered from certain bondages and brought by the Lord into tremendous liberty.

All that is wonderful, blessed indeed. I have no problem with the successes. The failures are my bother. My heart yearns over those who receive little, and even more so over those who received nothing.

What can be more hurtful than ministering to the cripple who desperately strives and even struggles in vain to stand, or to the blind who stumbles disappointedly away. Is there no healing from the Lord for all these?

This is a big question, but the answer is bound to be yes, there is! Then where is the operation of that faith as a grain of mustard seed of which our Saviour spoke?

It is quite clear that there is no rule of thumb for the operation of faith. George Muller used to be called the 'Nineteenth Century Apostle of Faith'. As I sit here in my house in Bristol, no more than a mile away are the majestic buildings which are a testimony to his faith in God. How he acquired the money to cover the cost of erecting and maintaining those splendid edifices was a secret little understood, apart from himself and his Maker.

Many may have tried to imitate Mr Muller, but to what end? "When money is sent to me for my own use" he used to say, "I pass it on to God." The more he sacrificed to God the more he received. So he did not need to hold onto any money. He simply used it all for the promotion of God's interests, and in so doing this man overcame all financial difficulties with a free heaven-backed flow of capital, most often from undisclosed sources.

He needed to have money to finance the scheme which in his heart he believed was of God, that of housing and caring for the many orphans of his day. He did not have to go to any other than the Lord for help. It was He who gave the vision in the first place. So he looked to Him alone, as he committed himself to the task.

Surely this man's faith was strong. How can we acquire this? The Bible says "Whatsoever is born of God overcometh the world: and this is the victory that overcometh the world, even our faith." Mr Muller obviously reckoned himself an overcomer of circumstances which are concerned with the world, and it behoves us to do the same. He recognized that money and all the world systems are subject to the Lord of Glory. And in applying himself daily to be in contact and communion with the Lord over matters of their mutual interest, the desired results were always at hand.

The mountains that seem impossible to us and are impossible to the nominal Christian, are bound to yield to the Holy Spirit engendered words of the man on his knees before his God.

It is only as we are faced with impossibilities that we sense our lack. How often some of us ask God for faith to remove mountains, and when He puts us in front of a mountain we go all to pieces! Clothed with the power of the Holy Spirit in the name of Jesus we really must speak to the mountains of today, and see them removed, if ever we should expect to possess the faith for tackling the mountains of tomorrow.

CHAPTER NINE

GIVE US A NEW START

God always speaks to faith. He is building a people of such a character with whom He can speak through His Word.

Where does faith begin? It begins with God. The Scriptures affirm 'Faith cometh by hearing, and hearing by the Word of God' (Rom. 10:17). When He speaks into our hearts this creates the faith which will never retreat nor recognize any barrier — overcoming faith.

We could never have lived nearly two thousand years ago like the apostles or others of that first Christian Church. We could never have had their particular calling, their faith, their power, but we have the same God. He is up to date. We 'Are come to the Kingdom for such a time as this' (Esther 4:14). This is the time when God needs us as co-workers with Him for as it were 'rounding off the age' — heralding the return of the Good Shepherd.

As we come with a true heart into God's presence confessing our unbelief, He will give us a new start. He alone knows how often this proves necessary. Would it not be marvellous if we could be commended like the Thessalonians 'your faith groweth exceedingly'.

Some ask, should we not seek to exercise love rather

than faith? This is understandable. Most of us are and should be concerned about the harrowing results of man's hate for man which are all around us. But let us not forget what the Bible says — 'without faith it is impossible to please Him (God)'. We will profit from holding things in their right perspective.

The Lord Jesus was also very much concerned about people's hatred for one another, and so were the apostles after Him. Did not He, as well as they, exercise love in all their ministry? Love, however does not operate without faith, nor does faith without love. God has already connected us to the latter. The Bible speaks of us as 'rooted and grounded in love'.

God does not ask us to love everybody because He loves the world. He wants us to love with His love. You would probably find it impossible to love me, but it is not so with God. He loves me all the time, and when you begin to love me with His love it is easy. We do not go to one another then to seek love, we go to God.

God is love and that love must be expressed. He expresses His love to us and we love one another through Him. Consequently we do not seek people to love us, but rather we seek to love them, for love 'seeketh not her own' (1 Cor. 13:5).

Character is what is going to matter in the eternal day, not so much what we have done, but what we are. "By this shall all men know that ye are my disciples, if ye have love one to another," said our Lord. The Christian Church has known this for nearly 2,000 years, and yet we have isms and schisms, and backbitings with us all the time. Surely if there is any place in the world where love should be manifest it should be in the house of God? There is so much talk of love these days, but some of this can adequately be called lust, which is quite a different thing from the love of which Jesus speaks. Sad to say that the former kind is noticeably creeping into the Church. The Gospel of Jesus Christ, however, presents us with a different type of living; a new and better quality to life, a life adjusted by the presence and power of the Holy Spirit.

It is shown in 1 Corinthians 13 what real love is. Love is not puffed up, it is not selfish, it does not behave unseemly, thinks no evil, not easily provoked, rejoices in the truth. The Bible says this kind of love is shed abroad in our hearts by the Holy Ghost, love that is without dissimulation, not an imitation.

There is also a natural love, common to the world. A man may love his own children dearly, but at the same time hate somebody else's. The Christian loves his own also other people's. 1 Peter 1:22 speaks of this love as 'unfeigned'. It is sincere, it is true, it is the love that was seen in Jesus Christ when wicked men pummelled and battered Him almost beyond recognition. He said "Father, forgive them; for they know not what they do."

We cannot love like this without the Spirit of Christ dwelling in us. This is the genuine love from heaven which promotes service to others.

Without the Holy Spirit then the whole Church is dead. It does not matter whether it is dead in the nicest ecclesiastical way, it is still dead. We the Church, the first born from the dead; represent the life of Christ, not some of it, the whole life — all of it settled legally at Calvary. We do not attain to anything God has given us. We only need to do what He says for He is committed to bring His own Word to pass.

All that is in the Word of God will not come to

fruition, will not come to pass for us individually or collectively, until we act upon it, for God has spoken. We cannot ask Him for further revelation than this. He is not going to give us any more. All He needs to do now is to reveal to us the truth of what He has already said, and this He will do as we begin to move by Holy Ghost faith.

The Bible does not say, 'now faith was'. Neither does it say, 'it is going to be'. Faith is the substance and the very foundation of effectiveness. The tragedy with many Christians though, is that as soon as they reach a certain level of spiritual maturity they cease to progress, they settle down. The same is true of many churches and movements that are now no more than mere monuments, broken shells of would-be spiritual strongholds. There came a time when the leaders of such churches or movements became satisfied. They became complacent; and in some instances quite unconsciously applied the brakes to the very organism which might have been to this day, under the regulation of the Holy Spirit, a live and vibrant witness unto the Lord of Glory.

Many of us take an unconscious pride in showing our lack of effectiveness. How often we say to people 'do not look at us, we have nothing to offer!' But it was not so with Peter, of whom James might well have written, as he did of Elijah, a man of like passions as ourselves. Peter boldly said "look on us . . . in the name of Jesus Christ of Nazareth . . . ." Might this not account for the difference in results.

Peter went on to explain the secret of his successful ministry. Infused with the Holy Spirit's power and ability the words of Jesus were just ringing in his heart 'freely you have received, freely give'. Our Saviour led captivity captive and gave gifts to men — to us — see Ephesians 4:8. A new start is a new start after all, new power, new vision, new gifts. They are all ours by the abiding presence of the Holy Spirit. We are Christ's witnesses. Not you in your small corner, and I in mine; corporate, recognizable witnesses.

Check the Scripture record of the first Corinthian Church. It received the baptism in the Holy Spirit. It had love, it had faith, it had power, and shared these with a needy world.

There is a dying world outside gasping, as it were, for the life-giving Word. How is it going to receive this Word? When in our teaching, preaching, or whatever ministry, we begin to speak words that are spirit and are life: words which by their very nature of being clothed upon by the Holy Spirit's power cannot be deflected by the Enemy from the hearts of the needy.

The body of Christ upon earth is expected to be so capacitated. At Pentecost it was ushered in, in such a blaze of glory. If it had continued like that the picture would have been different today. There certainly would not be so many divisions, so many walls, so many wranglings that can only weaken and dissipate our spiritual energy. Unity is strength. Divisiveness is weakness.

Looking back over the history of the Church it is sad that division has been allowed to such an extent that there are some Christians today who will not even as much as acknowledge others from other Churches. But Christ is not divided. If only we had learned this and stood together, many more millions would have come to Jesus Christ. We, like the early Christians, would have been hearing others saying "see how they love one another."

Many would-be Christians are looking to us, fully persuaded that they would be plunged into a life of gloom if they turn to Christ. Can they be blamed? As far as they are concerned it is an untried way of life, and if we are not really enjoying it they are not likely to. I believe the Holy Spirit is bent on correcting this situation. We are heaven's advertisement. No wonder Jesus prayed 'that your joy may be full', this is His longing. The Holy Spirit wants to exhibit Him as the chief corner-stone 'which the builders refused' but 'is become the head stone of the corner' (Psalm 118:22).

CHAPTER TEN

THE FULL GOSPEL

God has given us the unity of the Holy Spirit. As we draw closer to Him and to one another we are moving in the Truth which is making us free. His will for us is of the utmost good, and He wants to bring His redeemed people out of all oppression into 'the glorious liberty of the sons of God'.

The sons of God are free and nothing less. Firstly, we are free from sin. The Bible says 'sin shall not have dominion over us'. In other words we no longer have to sin as a matter of course. Having received forgiveness of sins what could be more joyous than to be walking in this newness of life? Once we were slaves unto sin, and could not help violating God's laws. But now we can say from grateful hearts, thank God for Jesus who has ransomed us.

His purposes as far as we are concerned are never seen through churchianity, denominationalism, or forms of worship, but by the direction which His people are taking, showing or giving.

It is well to remember that God has entrusted many notable tasks to us, His Church. When the early Church spoke people took notice, because the Church spoke with heaven's authority and power. They were a people who had their needs solved. The Scriptures tell us that not one amongst them lacked. The new principles upon which their lives were founded were anything but earthly. They did not have to pretend to be different from others, they were. It was obvious. Suddenly these Christians had become so resourceful that their power-packed ministry with signs and wonders were affecting vast areas of their community.

The Church then is not here just for a moral issue. Many regard it simply as an institution for christening, marrying and burying. The enlightened Christian does not see things this way.

Let us all see things as they really are from God's point of view. The function of the Church of Jesus Christ is to minister Life and give direction. Speaking of life in this connection means the Full Gospel. The Good News for modern man. It is as good today as ever it was, not just the preaching, not just the teaching, but the effective presentation of all that is embodied in Jesus' ministry — salvation for the soul, the baptism in the Holy Spirit, and healing for the body. Nothing could be more necessary today than this. Instead, however, we have Christian churches, Christian projects, Christian teaching, Christian doctrine, theology, and even philosophy. Christianity really is none of these. Granted that we have exemplary liturgical ceremonies, but Christianity made alive by the baptism in the Holy Spirit is not a system, not a label, not a doctrine.

'For we are the circumcision, which worship God in the Spirit, and rejoice in Christ Jesus, and have no confidence in the flesh' (Phil. 3:3).

Many who are baptized in the Holy Spirit are having a hard time. It is not that they are specially chosen to suffer. Nor is it that they have not received this bona fide blessing. It is simply that they are still struggling with the flesh. They have not fully surrendered to the Holy Spirit: hence there is little or no spiritual progress.

The flesh is very persistent. It will wriggle and scream and find any excuse for not being put down. But the fact remains that the Holy Spirit and the flesh are incompatible. The flesh is always striving for the mastery. It is relentless in its efforts either to quench the Spirit or cause the individual to feel that he is out of favour with God, and might as well return to his former way of living.

How do we identify the flesh? The Word of God is our only help here being 'quick, and powerful, and sharper than any two-edged sword, piercing even to the dividing asunder of soul and spirit, and of the joints and marrow, and is a discerner of the thoughts and intents of the heart' (Heb. 4:12). Those human desires, motives and intentions that would rob us of our spiritual advance are common to man. The apostle Paul had to battle against them. We can afford to listen to him. He says "let the Word of Christ dwell in you richly." In other words, as the Word of Christ is occupying the chief place in our hearts it will filter out those fleshly hindrances along with everything else that would try to encumber. When Paul had reached 'wit's-end corner' in his struggles with the flesh he cried out "who shall deliver me from the body of this death?" Of course, the answer was not a million miles away. Most, if not all, Christians know that 'deliverance is of the Lord', as Daniel of old knew and proved, as Joseph knew and proved, as David knew and proved.

So Paul is coming out onto the boulevard of faith. Speaking of the body of this death he identifies a life-style which at long last he recognizes as incurably bad. No doctor, no psychiatrist, no specialist, to whom he might turn, none but the Great Physician. Anchoring his faith in His almighty power Paul completes his exclamation "I thank God through Jesus Christ our Lord!"

There is no hope for us nor for the nations, but Christ: the people of this country lack much, and is there any chance of a change for the better? I believe there is. God still has a vibrant witness here upon the earth vested in His people. The Bible speaks of His inheritance in the saints — 'Christ in you the hope of glory'. We possess the solution for the society all around us, which is collapsing morally, socially, politically and economically.

Jesus said we are "the salt of the earth" (Matt. 5:13). Salt has many desirable uses. It is pleasant to the taste and is also a preservative. Without the redeemed of the Lord in the world sin and all its consequences would prevail. It would hardly be a place for human beings. But the presence of the Holy Spirit in the world, because of us, is keeping the enemy, Satan, relatively subdued.

The more we seek the Lord, continue being filled with the Holy Spirit and in His power seek to dispossess the enemy of his stranglehold upon the nation, the more we shall prove our God. 'The Lord omnipotent reigneth'. By the Holy Spirit He wants everything that He is to be brought out into the open, that the ungodly might see that when they are dealing with the Church, they are in fact dealing with God. Referring to John 17 again makes this plain. Jesus prays there with overt passion 'That they all may be one; as Thou, Father, art in me, and I in Thee, that they also may be one in us:

that the world may believe that Thou hast sent me'.

It has been wisely said 'Where there is no vision, the people perish'. Without a Church vision from God, that Full Gospel of Jesus Christ by the power of the Holy Spirit, will never be realized up and down our land: that unifying spirit-healing, soul-healing, body-healing, all embracing gospel of peace and consolation. We need that vision. We need dreams too. Without them we shall perish. The baptism in the Holy Spirit and the attendant gifts are not given to us that we might sit back with a pious feeling of contentment. Having received all these we have not reached finality. Once we start thinking that we have, spiritual decline ensues.

Ephesians 4 shows us the goal upon which the Holy Spirit is focussing the Church's attention. "Till we all come in the unity of the faith, and of the knowledge of the Son of God, unto a perfect man, unto the measure of the stature of the fulness of Christ."

CHAPTER ELEVEN

REDUNDANT MINISTERS

Christ then, in all His fulness shall be manifested in the Church before His actual return. All His attributes shall be plainly recognizable in and amongst His people.

In fulness, 'as the waters cover the sea', so shall the glory of the Lord be seen covering the whole earth. Then and only then can Christ come, as the preparation of the bride by the Holy Spirit is brought to a conclusion, that which He has set out to accomplish in the Church. He shall present the Church to Christ as His bride 'not having spot, or wrinkle, or any such thing'. Christ 'shall see of the travail of His soul, and shall be satisfied', displaying her indeed to a wondering universe.

We can afford to take courage here, in that the Holy Spirit is not yet finished with any of us. That bride will be beautiful, perfect, despite what some of us might be thinking of ourselves at this moment. We might even be asking, are we really of bridal quality with all our faults and failings? No! But let us take note of what the Scripture says 'We all, with open face beholding as in a glass the glory of the Lord, are changed into the same image from glory to glory, even as by the Spirit of the Lord' (2 Cor. 3:18). He is making us into the most beautiful people in the world, a heavenly people, possessed of Christlikeness.

None of us knows exactly what things will be like when Christ appears, but we do know that we shall be like Him, for the Scriptures say so. This then is the time to progress, the vision in front of us being that wonderful measure of the incomparable stature. What does the Bible say? 'He that descended is the same also that ascended up far above all heavens, that He might fill all things and He gave some, apostles; and some, prophets; and some, evangelists; and some, pastors and teachers; for the perfecting of the saints, for the work of the ministry, for the edifying of the body of Christ' (Eph. 4:10).

Note the word 'perfecting'. This signifies a process, a moving forward on a progressive course. God has provided us with all that He deems necessary for our being perfect when His Son arrives to collect us for our eternal abode.

We are living in a day when we are going to see Jesus Christ as He really is, manifested. We are going to see angels, we shall see and be involved in many supernatural things that we have never encountered before. The world too shall see all that we love and have been contending for, demonstrated. God so loved the world that He gave us Christ. If ever we are to love and win the world for Him He has first to work in us the power to do for them what they cannot do for themselves. Love heals the sick, sets the people free. The Word becomes health to all their flesh.

We are moving into a time when there will not be any need of special prayers for anyone in our meetings. In fact, already there are many reports of people being healed and set free from many a disability without

E

anyone in particular ministering to them. The Holy
Spirit in doing this. The demons flee as He moves in
deliverance upon the people for whom Jesus Christ
died.

The Old Testament account of Solomon, the
building of the temple, and its dedication, is a good
example of what the Holy Spirit is doing within the
Church. In 1 Kings 1:6 we see that 'the house, when it
was in building, was built of stone made ready before it
was brought thither: so that there was neither hammer
nor axe nor any tool of iron heard in the house, while it
was in building'.

They were just natural stones out there in their
natural surroundings where they had always been until
the quarryers and masons intervened. Some of these
stones were large, others small; some were dark, others
light; some were heavy, others were not. What a
perfect example of the sons of men.

The Bible says first 'that which is natural; and
afterwards that which is spiritual' (1 Cor. 15:46). Born
of our mother, we too were just natural and remained
in our natural surroundings. None of us entered into
this life a regenerate child of God. It was by the work
of the Holy Spirit through human agency at some time
or other that secured us, made us ready, and set us in
the body of Christ. Why human agency? God does not
have any other way. He does nothing in the earth
without involving humanity. We are destined for an
eternal relationship. God is bound up with His
creation by word and deed. This is shown throughout
Scripture.

To name but a few examples of this we have only to
look at Genesis Chapter 6 where He wanted to bring a
flood upon the earth. What did He do? He called on

Noah and confided this to him; and in Genesis Chapter 18 He wanted to destroy Sodom and Gomorrah. He called on His 'friend' Abraham and discussed this with him. And in Chapter 13 of Judges where He wanted to begin to deliver the Israelites from the Philistines, He called on Manoah and his wife. God never acts autocratically.

Taking a further look at the temple, we too are stones, 'lively stones' which are not being built into an earthly temple as those were, but a heavenly, by the Holy Spirit. The record shows that the temple was raised up in silence. This in itself is marvellous, showing that what the Holy Spirit is doing with the Church is not making headline news in the world. His work is like that of leaven in dough. We cannot see how the leaven is achieving its effect, yet the results are manifest.

But of even greater significance is this fact. When Solomon was dedicating the completed building the glory of the Lord filled the entire house, so much so that no one could minister — no priest — just the glory of the LORD, filling the whole house. The ministers were instantly redundant. This is so beautifully pictorial, showing as it does this wonderful consummation, Christ being all and in all. What fulfillment!

God has promised to fill this latter house with greater glory than the former. Has He a house to fill? Has He a temple? We are His holy habitation, and the Holy Spirit is the Master Builder, that Solomon of all ages. He is completing a building of which He shall not be ashamed. He does not have to work according to drawings prepared by architects or surveyors. And there is no fear of any substandard material slipping through into the building to mar its perfection. He does not have to check for errors in the plans. The plans were made and agreed among the Father, Son and Holy Spirit before errors were ever possible, before the foundation of the world.

God shall have a people upon the earth enjoying the full benefits of Calvary. Some 'God-sized' benefits are awaiting us from heaven. Illustrating this in Matthew 7:11, Jesus comments on how some parents give unstintingly to their children. He goes on to say "How much more shall your Father which is in heaven give good things to them that ask Him?"

Moses had to build according to the pattern that he had seen on the mount. That was an excellent pattern: God's own design. But it was only a shadow of the magnificent habitation of God that the Holy Spirit is currently erecting. His pattern is none other than God's Son.

We look at ourselves and are often disappointed. We are weak even feeble at times. We feel totally incapable of facing any challenge. This is good. These are important qualities, which are necessary for this wonderful Church. It is not what we are but who He is that matters. We have to let Him into every aspect of our life. His life has already overcome all that we shall ever need to overcome — sin, sickness, disease, demon power, lack of money, circumstances . . . the list is endless. This is the victorious life that He has given us. We can have as much of it as we want. 'In all things we are more than conquerors through Him that loved us'.

What about joy? A great many people do not appear to be as joyous nowadays as they might be. The people of God should never be lacking in this. 'The joy of the Lord is our strength'. As we wait upon Him His heart is made joyous and we reap the benefit, strength.

It is doubtful whether many of us appreciate what this really means. We are ineffective and desperately in need of the Lord's help. Consequently, we tend to relate needs solely to human beings. But if only we could see that God our Father also has needs, this would make all the difference. In the light of the Scripture in front of us 'His joy' which He experiences by virtue of our response to Him 'is our strength'.

What strength do we need? Strength to pray, to exercise faith, patience, love . . . . The whole point is that we are dependent upon God and He is dependent upon us. His strength is made perfect in weakness. According to 2 Corinthians 12:9 this is what the Apostle Paul heard from God. We can then without fear of contradiction say that our weakness is an aid to God's perfection. He needs our weakness and we need His strength. His plan of creation is just that, and will culminate in everything that has breath praising the Lord (see Psalm 150).

Continuing on the theme of God's relationship with man: when God created Adam and Eve the first thing He did was to establish a relationship between them and Himself. He now had two human beings with whom He could commune.

The Bible records that God used to visit them during the cool of the day. That was precious. He was having enjoyable fellowship with His intelligent creation. True it was not long before the Devil spoiled that relationship when he managed to deceive Eve, causing both herself and her husband to disobey God. And what a catastrophe that was! What a loss to God, but in Christ — the last Adam — He has regained more than He lost in the first. Have you ever thought that it was a tremendous blessing to the human race, that God banned Adam and his wife from the Garden of Eden, once they had transgressed His commandment? Suppose they had been allowed to continue there in their sin and then eat of the Tree of Life. All their descendents including ourselves would have remained in sin for ever, separated from the Lord. There would never have been the slightest opportunity of knowing God as Father, or Jesus as Saviour, or the Holy Spirit as the Comforter, the Uniting bond of Peace.

God has in Christ rescued us from the fall. The Holy Spirit attests to this. 'Behold my servant, whom I uphold; mine elect, in whom my soul delighteth; I have put my Spirit upon Him: He shall bring forth judgement to the Gentiles'. However weak we may find ourselves, because of Jesus this can be, as it were, a spring-board to strength. The Holy Spirit's focus of attention on Him through us delights the heart of our Father. Love must triumph. The Father loves the Son and has given all things into His hands. The Son having brought many sons unto Him — the many (ourselves) whom He has redeemed from the fall, He has equipped with new vision, new power, new gifts. We are living witnesses unto Him throughout our land.

This is the abundant life, indeed 'joy unspeakable and full of glory'. So there is never any need of asking God for joy. Not that we would receive it anyway. Living in the benefits of the Full Gospel we simply experience Jesus' promise in John 15:11 "These things have I spoken unto you, that my joy might remain in you, and that your joy might be full." And what is the result of this fullness? "Speaking to yourselves in psalms and hymns and spiritual songs, singing and making melody in your heart to the Lord" (Eph. 5:19).

People who are full of joy have no place for

boredom and misery. They have finished with such things. King David must have arrived at this. He said "Enter into His gates with thanksgiving, and into His courts with praise: be thankful unto Him, and bless His name" (Psalm 100:4).

By all accounts this man had reached a state of spiritual maturity wherein he could start every day alike, praising the Lord, not just when the weather was fine and all circumstances congenial. For him, God's mercies were new every morning. Surely this is how we should all be, rejoicing in hope; even in persecution.

CHAPTER TWELVE

THE SUPER-NATIONAL FAMILY

'Be glad in the Lord, and rejoice, ye righteous: and shout for joy, all ye that are upright in the heart' says Psalm 32:11.

Some of us say we do not feel like rejoicing. That does not matter. If we had to wait for our feelings to register our spiritual state before we obeyed the Lord's commands of love, we would never enjoy much of the benefits of our present salvation. Our feelings are often like the weather — unstable. But when we remember what the Lord has done for us, deep down in our hearts there is that tremendous response of love which keeps us aglow with desire for Him.

He is the centre of our thoughts and affections. So rejoicing in Him is a matter of obedience and love. The sacrifice of praise is costly. Praising and rejoicing go hand in hand. David said "I will not take that which is thine for the Lord, nor offer burnt offerings without cost" (1 Chron. 21:24). God has in Christ provided us with the ability to respond to Him in every way that His relationship with us demands. 'By Him (Christ) therefore let us offer the sacrifice of praise to God continually, that is, the fruit of our lips giving thanks to His name' (Heb. 13:15).

Have you ever seen a sad person praising the Lord?

According to the Bible, in a time of recession (economic depletion) there is rejoicing for God's people. "Although the fig tree shall not blossom, neither shall fruit be in the vines;" says Habbakkuk . . . "yet I will rejoice in the Lord, I will joy in the God of my salvation."

There is no inflation in heaven; no Chancellor of the Exchequer, no drought nor rain, no deprivation whatever. What manner of people ought we to be, seeing that the things that are all around us will be dissolved very soon. We belong to a 'super-national' family — sons of God by regeneration. Put in another way we belong to one Father, even God, and are 'all of One', as the Scriptures say.

Here in the world we have the comfort of the Father, Son and Holy Spirit to make us 'super-conquerors'. The things that assail us such as tribulation, distress, persecution, famine . . . we meet at wit's-end corner. To date not many of us have encountered all of these. Nevertheless, we are 'persuaded, that neither death, nor life, nor angels, nor principalities, nor powers, nor things present, nor things to come, nor height, nor depth, nor any other creature, shall be able to separate us from the love of God, which is in Christ Jesus our Lord' (Rom. 8:38-39).

In the first Christian Church the people were found 'rejoicing that they were counted worthy to suffer shame for His (Christ's) name' (Acts 5:41).

Did they have a different baptism from that which we received? — that is doubtful — although the circumstances in which we receive matter much. Some of us lay great store by this blessing, as a goal in itself — a fulfilment that will satisfy a certain definite need. Either we were not taught correctly or do not understand that this is far from the truth. We receive, speak a few or many words in tongues, and the brakes are applied.

Who can challenge the fact that there is a wonderful change in our lives. We are much more spiritually aware than we had been. Yet, for some reason or other there is not that distinguishing spiritual dynamic about us which even remotely resembles any of the characters who were baptized in the Holy Spirit on the day of Pentecost.

What is missing? The power — it is either not received, not evident, or stifled. So we are well advised to check on whether our experience measures up to Matthew 3:11 'He shall baptize you with the Holy Ghost, and with fire: whose fan is in His hand, and He will thoroughly purge His floor, and gather His wheat into the garner; but He will burn up the chaff with unquenchable fire'.

We have said much about receiving and using power from on high, how many of us realize that in a certain sense power on its own is not much good without the authority to execute it? A steam engine might be full of power as it stands in one position. Its movement from point A to point B depends on the release of that power. All the time that it is standing it is accomplishing no useful purpose. Does this awaken your imagination? It is so easy to be found running on the spot.

A certain friend of mine had had a mighty baptism in the Holy Spirit and his life was manifestly transformed. Whereas he used to read his Bible and long for revelation on what he was reading, now the revelation was just streaming in from heaven. His prayers too were different. They were lively and of a high spiritual tone, and he was obviously more loving and tender-hearted to everybody. As far as he was concerned he felt that he had received a mandate from God to share His salvation with the whole world. Burning with zeal he was convinced that under his hands great numbers would come into the benefits of the full Gospel.

There was certainly nothing wrong with such noble convictions. Nor was there anything wrong with his visitation from heaven, but like that steam engine, he was running on the spot. By the end of thirty-three days my friend began to feel disillusioned. Why? No one appeared to want anything that he was offering. He was telling out the good message to all and sundry with no apparent results for the Kingdom of God. It was at this point that he realized that something was lacking.

The Bible tells us what this was. He had zeal, he had the coveted 'power', he had courage, and enthusiasm, but it was 'the zeal of the Lord of Hosts' that would perform this. My friend dropped to his knees before God and cried unto Him afresh. It was during this talk with His Maker that he was going to receive that authority, that release of the Spirit which would bring him into ministering effectively. Shortly afterwards this man was leading many to Christ and ministering healing to many a folk. God would have us all to be 'able ministers of the New Testament'.

It is very easy to become a Christian. All one has to do is to repent of one's sins and put one's faith in God for salvation through Jesus Christ. After that it is easy to receive the baptism in the Holy Spirit. All we have to do is to ask of Jesus the Baptizer and we will receive this inestimable blessing. But it is not so easy to live like

Jesus, to be a minister of righteousness, of peace, of love, of health, of comfort, consolation . . .

Before we can be used by God we must be shaped to His liking. We can hardly fail to see this as we examine Revelations 1:10 which speaks so blessedly of the apostle John's experience. Nobody could have been more in the Spirit than he was. He testifies "I was in the Spirit on the Lord's day." And on what better day could this have been. This was either a Monday, or a Tuesday, Wednesday . . . . Then someone spoke to him. This is tremendous. When a man is in the Spirit 'Someone' (the Lord) always speaks to him. John turned round to see the One who had spoken "And when I saw Him" said John, "I fell at His feet as dead."

This deadness was vital to the task that was soon to be given him, as we shall see. Verses 17 to 20 say "And He laid His right hand upon me, saying unto me, 'Fear not; . . . write the things which thou hast seen, and the things which are, and the things which shall be hereafter' . . . ."

What a commission that was! But note, John had first to be prostrate before the Lord. He had to feel and experience his own weakness — his own death — before he could receive the Divine energy for becoming a writer of God's precious Holy Word. Equipped by the Lord he would set down for posterity, the things that he would hear from Him.

To live in the Holy Spirit we have first to die. Paul boasts in 1 Corinthians 15:31 "I die daily." This presents tremendous difficulties to some of us. The Holy Spirit creates the hunger in our hearts for this, but somehow there is the flesh to contend with. For many would-be mighty men of God death in this particular sense is a very long and painful process.

God is God of the present. He is also progressive and our understanding of Him should be progressive. The hunger which the Holy Spirit engenders in us is such as will always bring us into line with the blessing of God. John 12:24 illustrates this 'Except a corn of wheat fall into the ground and die, it abideth alone: but if it die, it bringeth forth much fruit.'

We cannot voluntarily die to self. This dying is really the progressive will and work of our Heavenly Father, so that nothing of ourselves might remain. There must not be any obstacle to the life of Christ being manifested through us as human vessels.

Talking about hunger, it seems God would move earth and heaven to satisfy the hungry heart. Acts 10 tells us of a man who had a deep spiritual hunger. His name was Cornelius, an officer in the Roman army, a Gentile outside of the possibility of being blessed by God, as far as the Jews were concerned.

Some people are careless about spiritual matters, but not this man. The text shows that he was earnestly seeking, according to the light that he had. It is important to remember that in those days the Gospel was being preached to Jews only. The preachers were holding the glorious message of salvation within certain national limits. But as the Scriptures tell us 'the Word of God is not bound'. He and the hungry heart must get together.

God was concerned that Cornelius should be entirely satisfied — he should receive a message by the Holy Spirit that would cause his faith to be settled in Christ. There were far greater things in store for this man, he would come into the benefits of Calvary.

So God had to do a special work in the apostle Peter by way of a vision to get him to visit Cornelius with the

Good News. At the same time he also gave Cornelius a vision of Peter's arriving. And when Peter actually got to the house, having taken a party of his friends with him, he had the shock of his life. God was already in the place. There was already a meeting in progress. Verse 34 tells us what happened as Peter joined in and opening his mouth said "of a truth I perceive that God is no respector of persons: but in every nation he that feareth Him, and worketh righteousness is accepted with Him."

The text also shows us that up to this time the apostle had clean forgotten Jesus' injunction in Matthew 28 "Go ye therefore, and teach all nations . . . ." and the message that he himself preached at Pentecost regarding Joel's prophecy (see Acts 2:17). But God would not allow this lapse to continue much longer. Chapter 11:15 tells us what happened in this relation. "As I began to speak," said Peter "the Holy Ghost fell on them, as on us at the beginning. Then 'remembered' I the Word of the Lord, how that he said, John indeed baptized with water; but ye shall be baptized with the Holy Ghost."

When Peter heard these Gentile believers 'speak with tongues, and magnify God', he was astonished, so much so that he exclaimed 'can any man forbid water, that these should not be baptized, which have received the Holy Ghost as well as we?' Yes, Peter like many of us had to realize that God is blessing people we would not bless. The Holy Spirit is falling upon people in places of which some of us would not approve. These things are happening wherever men and women are listening to, and longing after God's Word. He is not afflicted with meanness, partiality or prejudice. On the contrary everybody can receive something from God.

We need not look for further explanation than we have in the New Testament for this assurance. It says 'repent, and be baptized every one of you in the name of Jesus Christ . . . and ye shall receive the gift of the Holy Ghost, for the promise is unto you . . .' (Acts 2:38). This is why we exhort the unsaved to receive the Lord Jesus, become a child of God (John 1:12), and receive the Holy Spirit. It is always a tragedy when a man dies in his sins, having missed, rejected or neglected the free gift of his Creator.

CHAPTER THIRTEEN

RESCUING THE PERISHING

Recently I read a book which described the life-style of a very famous actor who had died tragically a few months earlier. It was surprising to learn that he used to consult clairvoyants, spiritists and mystics for guidance for every important decision of his career. It is little wonder then, that after a very immoral life having had several wives, etc. while still a relatively young man he was cut off in his prime. And what did he leave? He left everything, including millions of pounds, valuable property and the memory of a life-style that shall never benefit anyone. As Jesus said "what shall it profit a man, if he shall gain the whole world (fame, riches, popularity . . .) and lose his own soul."

People are perishing, but God through Christ has raised up a rescue team by the Holy Spirit. Thank God for Jesus. We have the mind of Christ, 'in Him we live, and move, and have our being'.

What does the baptism in the Holy Spirit really demand of us? When we receive this blessing the things that are not suited to our life of witnessing unto our Saviour are soon gone. People sometimes worry about the cost to themselves. They think about the golf, the drink, the smoking, the club life, the wining and dining, romancing and gambling. How are we going to forsake all this? they say. Obviously they are not thinking of all that they are going to gain. The word power, has not yet become meaningful to such people. It has not yet become part of their language and consciousness.

Remember the Holy Spirit is not the author of boredom, routine or monotony. All this comes from the human spirit. We create this just as we create the divisions in the Church. Now, talking about the Full Gospel clearly implies that there is a half Gospel and a quarter Gospel and a . . . . We give such a poor witness to a world that so needs the full orbed Gospel, the 'Good News for Modern Man'. Without this fullness of presentation of Christ as Saviour, Healer, Baptizer in the Holy Spirit, our witness is lacking.

It is so easy to instruct on doctrine, ceremony, ecclesiastical propriety, and even churchianity, and forget the power of the Holy Spirit to make Christ real. What is any preaching worth without Him? It is the Holy Spirit's prerogative to make Him attractive to the sinner. The whole world without Christ is under condemnation. "And this is the condemnation," says John 3:19,20, "that light is come into the world, and men loved darkness rather than light, because their deeds were evil. For every one that doeth evil hateth the light, neither cometh to the light, lest his deeds should be reproved." So people are not automatically seeking the Saviour. They are in fact keeping away from Him as our text here shows. But the Holy Spirit through us would lighten their darkness.

In this sense then we are taking over the world for Jesus. Like the prophet of old we have a mantle of power that fell on us from on high, eclipsing all our weaknesses and enabling us to rescue the perishing.

F

The power of God cannot be equalled. According to the Scriptures there are some people who have a 'form of Godliness, but denying the power thereof' (2 Tim. 3:5). What does this mean? They have not really been regenerate. They are not just weak. They have not genuinely received the power for Christian living. They call themselves Christians because they have joined the Church, and are active in Christian service, and labours of all kinds, Missionary endeavours, Sunday Schools, and so on. They give their money to the Church — their time and efforts all centre around Christianity. Every outward appearance is good. They have a form of godliness. What does the Bible say about these? It is very clear on this matter. 'From such turn away' (2 Tim. 3:5). Do not have fellowship with them. They are the type who feel that they really need 'a religion'. They need their consciences eased.

They are the kind of people whom God said are for ever learning and are never able to come to a knowledge of the Truth. How do we identify them? 'By their fruits you shall know them'. They have not the power to witness unto the risen Christ, and this is the real trouble. We do not have to go very far to meet one of these kind good-natured people, in the local church perhaps, or somewhere else. He speaks affectionately of . . . the Bible of his childhood days, which he tells us cannot now be wholly accepted as the truth, since we have become more educated. Of course, he might explain, science has thrown much light on hitherto misunderstood Scripture.

And again, we are sure to meet another who says, "Well the Gospel works for some people, but certainly not for everybody. With the advance in technology and science only some parts of the Bible are credible today. A loving God as some preachers portray would never allow so much trouble in the world, so much suffering . . . .''

So God says these folk are ever learning and to what end? Resisting the truth — men of corrupt minds, reprobate concerning the faith.

The Bible also speaks of some who even have another Jesus, as outlined in 2 Cor. 11:4 'For if he that cometh preacheth another Jesus, whom we have not preached, or if ye receive another spirit, which ye have not received, or another gospel, which ye have not accepted . . . .' Mark you, they are very plausible. They will tell us that Jesus was the greatest preacher, the greatest teacher, the greatest human being that ever lived: indeed, the greatest social worker, a man of miracles and tremendous love.

Would they ever acknowledge Him as Christ and Saviour, the eternal Son of God, the Creator of the Universe and Baptizer in the Holy Spirit, the Healer — for themselves? They put forward a Jesus who is a great man — in a certain sense one of the greatest of the sons of God, revealing Himself in such marvellous humanitarian ways. He is, they might tell us, one whom we should follow, and there is nothing to compare with His Sermon on the Mount . . . .

For ourselves, we know that most of these things are true — wonderfully true. But we do not have to be spiritually bright to see that there is something sadly lacking, gravely deceptive in all this. The Lord Jesus is not acknowledged as He really is. The whole of His Divinity is undermined.

Let us test all these people and their motives by Scripture. Jesus asked Peter a vital question "Whom say ye that I am?" (Matt. 16:15) "Thou are the Christ, the Son of the living God" he responded.

This was no slick answer from the man whom many justifiably dub impetuous. Nor was this a wild guess. There was definite Holy Ghost guidance behind every word that he uttered in regard of the Saviour. This was tremendous revelation; so much so that Jesus had to comment, "Flesh and blood hath not revealed it unto thee, but my Father which is in heaven."

Was it not wonderful, some of us might say, that Peter on this particular occasion did not fail Jesus? Was it? Rather was it not precious that the power of the LORD was there to single out the Son of the Most High. May God grant us the abiding presence of that power. We would do well to consider that Old Testament character called Obadiah and what he did. He did not appear to understand spiritual warfare and the liberality of God. At a time of tremendous crisis we see this man powerlessly cringing from the enemy. Talking to Elijah he tried to justify himself and his position, "Was it not told my Lord what I did when Jezebel slew the prophets of the LORD," he said, "how I hid an hundred men of the LORD'S prophets by fifty in a cave, and fed them with bread and water?" (1 Kings 18:13).

Obadiah was proud of what he had done. But what a tragedy that was! Just at the crucial time when these, would-be valuable men of God, were most needed out there on the battlefield to proclaim the Word of the Lord; giving direction and raising up a standard against the enemy; they were rendered impotent, being locked away in a cave, of all places. How sad! God save us from the Obadiahs of today who, under the pretext of ultra godliness, would shield God's prophets from service in this the day of battle. It is high time for the prophets of the Lord to be heard in our lands dealing a sweeping blow to the gross spiritual ignorance that abounds. We shall come to this again.

There was nothing wrong with Obadiah's relationship with the Lord as far as we know. On the contrary, 'he feared the Lord greatly'. But being right with the Lord and hearing from heaven to the benefit of others and the Church are not one and the same. We can be so right in ourselves and before God, faithful, yet without any evidence of Holy Ghost power.

The mention of the bread and water is highly significant. His vision of God's provision for His people was miniscule. What Obadiah did not seem to realize was that God was able for every situation. His provision for His people does not depend on circumstances, and is infinitely more than bread and water.

Is it not beautiful how Elijah handles this matter? He appears to ignore what Obadiah has said and declares that despite all circumstances he would face the enemy. "As the LORD of Hosts liveth before whom I stand, I will surely show myself unto him (King Ahab) today." The difference between this man's perception of God and Obadiah's was remarkable. Elijah's God was not mean, the God of Hosts he called Him. What does this mean?

He is God of all Hosts wherever and whatever they might be — hosts of angels, hosts of stars, hosts of friends, hosts — even of enemies, visible and invisible. He is over them all. He is the Omnipotent One, God of the Universe who is always capable of making a way where there is no way. The battle was His, as far as

Elijah was concerned.

Let us beware of ministering respectability for spirituality. However good or moral the social standards and principles are, they will never stand in place of God's Word. In the presence of the Lord we live in an entirely different atmosphere and this difference should manifest itself wherever we happen to be.

Obadiah was a respectable man, certainly not a man of straw. But the prophet treated him the same as anyone else. All too often some of us are guilty of taking far too much care of embarrassing people instead of telling them the plain truth. Whether they are of high or low estate, people need the incisive edge of 'the Sword of the Spirit', instead of a shield. This is exactly what Elijah demonstrated on coming face to face with the wicked King Ahab. Elijah rebuked him for a second time for his idolatry with no deference to his being the sovereign (See 1 Kings 17 & 18).

'Follow after charity', we are exhorted in 1 Corinthians 14, 'and desire spiritual gifts, but rather that ye may prophesy'. We desperately need the prophets of the Lord who will say the things that God wants them to say, and not what the people want to hear. God is raising up such prophets. The spirit that motivated His servant Elijah is not dead. Expect prophecies and expect to prophesy, these being the last of the last days. The time has come for God's people to rise up with their eyes on the target. And what is that? The coming of the Lord draweth nigh. For far too long we have been afflicted with folk who are refusing to engage in open warfare with the enemy.

Who is a prophet? He is essentially a man anointed of God with the Holy Ghost and power to deliver God's

Word to the peoples and the nations.

Look at God's natural children. They are coming into their land and preparing for their Messiah, but we must prepare for the Bridegroom. Remember them fighting their enemies just a few years ago? Israel was threatened and what did she do? She struck first, and, as it happened, kept well within the customary law — six days fighting and the battle was won and over. So they could rest on the seventh day.

There is a vital lesson in this for the Church today and indeed for all of us. We need the prophet's word. He must be around to announce where we might strike first. The enemy should never be given an opportunity to harass us. We should be giving him a hard time, as a result of our hearing from heaven, the source of our ability.

CHAPTER FOURTEEN

BEING IN TUNE

We are not relying on natural forces. Neither is it a battle of wits between us and the enemy.

From his side, Satan (the Devil) marshalls his forces with great skill and tactics which we cannot, and should not try to equal. Was it not in this very matter that King David once greatly erred? He had had much experience with God and knew that his power and ability came from Him. Yet we see that David lost his spiritual stance by numbering Israel. He counted all the able bodied men who could fight just to be sure of how many he had.

There is a tremendous lesson for us here. May God grant that we continually listen to the "'Voice' of His word" as the Scriptures put it, so that we are never caught off guard as David was. Many of us would think David knew and trusted God to be his defence. Surely, we may say, he knew the goodness of the Lord from the Goliath episode; and from his adventure with the lion and the bear; and his tremendous escapades with King Saul . . . . Yet, 1 Chronicles 21:1 says 'Satan stood up against Israel, and provoked David to number Israel.'

This was the crux of the whole matter, and how often this stance that the Enemy takes up against the people of God proves equally crucial for us today. He is never far away and is always ready to take advantage of any situation for dissuading us from what is right in the Lord.

Obviously David did not recognize Satan's stratagem. It was just as though he was suddenly struck with spiritual blindness. We must never underestimate the value of these Scriptures which are ever ready to hand as our guide. Thank God for the Holy Spirit who is so insistent on maintaining us in the glow of His presence, as we yield to Him.

Satan will never force us to do anything. He does not have the ability to do this, as we are no longer his slaves. He never forced David. He only presented him with the temptation. From the Scriptures we know what to do when these times arise. 'Submit yourselves therefore to God', says James 4:7. 'Resist the Devil, and he will flee from you'. So much depends on this submitting. On the occasion in question, if only David had given himself and his affairs over to the Lord all would have been well.

Even his Captain Joab could see that things were not going to turn out well for Israel. It is recorded that he cautioned his master that God was well able to make whatever number they were sufficient for any battle. But, as the record shows, something that is typical in the lives of many today happened. David made up his own mind. He counted his men who were suited for war. Regardless of any consideration to the contrary he would make sure that his forces were equal to the enemy's. How sad! This gross act of folly was very costly. Instead of victory over the enemy David brought down the very wrath of the Almighty not only on himself but also on the people under him. In the words of the Bible 'God was displeased with this thing;

therefore He smote Israel'.

The Bible says 'there hath no temptation taken you but such as is common to man: but God is faithful, who will not suffer you to be tempted above that ye are able; but will with the temptation also make a way to escape, that ye may be able to bear it'. Could King David have escaped doing what he did? Was there a way provided for him to bear it?

Joab is not usually regarded as a prophet of the Lord. But who can gainsay the fact that he prophesied during that tremendous crisis of David's apparent spiritual lapse. Joab was used of God to justify His name by warning David against the impending error. This is wonderfully encouraging that in temptation's hour God is always so concerned for our well-being that He provides a way out for us. Did not the Lord Jesus teach us to pray 'lead us not into temptation, but deliver us from evil'?

In itself temptation is not sin. Often some well-meaning Christians are over-occupied with this. Because the enemy puts temptation in their way they tend to think that they are the worst sinners around. They ought to be encouraged to read what is said in James 1:2,3 'Count it all joy when you fall into diverse temptations; knowing this, that the trying of your faith worketh patience.' We must be tested, we must be tried. God loves us too much to leave us to our own devices. We would never develop any spiritual muscles, but for the trials and temptations.

One of the temptations to which many easily fall prey is to rely on experience. In spiritual matters however precious the experience, that is all it is, and nothing more. Under the hand of God we might heal the sick, bring many to a saving knowledge of Christ and even raise the dead. We may be responsible for the removal of many a mountain and hill; and the exalting of many a valley. But none of these things can ever happen automatically. At all times we must be hearing from heaven, or else we, like David, shall surely find that the enemy has subtly taken us off course. And as we have already seen the tragedy is that we are not the only ones who suffer the consequences.

There is really no substitute for being in unison with heaven. Then and only then can we be sure that the blessing of God will follow us.

Some of us tend to be caught up with the euphoria of the Charismatics; typical of these times, with the notion that that is all there is to Christian living. Let us hasten to add, that there is nothing wrong with this beautiful work of God. No one can deny the benefits of being caught up in the presence of the Lord; in the fervour of singing and dancing, and praising. Those of us who have experienced, and are experiencing, this liberty in the Holy Spirit should be grateful to God for this is very precious, having special regard for the fact that God inhabits the 'praises of His people'.

Nevertheless, let it be far from us that we should ever be caught — as is reported of some — neglecting His Word. Its importance is all pervading. As we have been seeing, listening to God's Word gives balance, stability, direction, correction and guidance.

For example, King David was having a tremendous time one day. He was engaged in a very noble act, bringing the Ark from the camp of the Philistines back to the camp of Israel. The Glory of the LORD had for a long time departed: Ichabod had taken It's place (See 1 Samuel 4:21).

David had gathered the singers the musicians and a

great crowd of people. After all, this was a really great
Convention and David and the folk danced, shouted
and praised the Lord.

They truly had something to shout about and
nothing should have stopped them for their hearts
were really set on doing what was right. But, there in
the midst of all that was going on, tragedy struck. A
man suddenly fell dead, all because they had not
heeded the Word of God. In the heat of the moment
"Uzza put forth his hand to hold the ark; for the oxen
stumbled."

There was nothing wrong with the tremendous time
they were having; nothing wrong with the music or the
shouting or the dancing, but there was everything
wrong with what Uzza did. Praise and worship are
absolutely necessary, speaking in tongues is necessary;
let us have all these things — everything in its right
order. Amidst all this there must be keenly listening
ears to the Word of God. It is a precious realization
that here in a particular sense was the Glory of the
LORD being brought back into Its right place through
the good offices of His servant David. For ourselves, we
are living in a peculiarly wonderful age when the Glory
of the LORD is truly coming back into Its place.

God help us to keep our hands off! It is better for us
to be live witnesses to Jesus our Lord than to be dead
heroes.

All is well if the Holy Spirit is the leader in these
things. He will never lead us awry. When our hands
are clean and holy before God, then we can lift them
up and praise the Lord.

Some may ask, does this mean that we need to listen
to more preaching or teaching of God's Word? Not
necessarily to either. As we continually seek Him, daily

reading the Bible for ourselves, talking with the Lord, and having fellowship with His people, He will speak to us.

Many great men of renown have sadly lost their way and the memory of their lives is a blessing to no one. We have only to examine the 'Hall of Fame' as portrayed in Hebrews 11 to see the contrast in Enoch, Noah, Abraham, Joseph . . . . If we are really in tune with heaven when God speaks we are never in doubt of His voice or of what He says. Do you remember the Mount Carmel episode detailed in 1 Kings 18 and the aftermath. A look at those happenings soon show us that God's speaking with us does not depend on circumstances, events, the time of day or night, but upon our openness of heart and willingness to hear.

Elijah the prophet was feeling very dejected, depressed and even fearful. Some of us might readily identify with him in his sad state. If ever anyone needed to hear from God this man did. As he sat musing God intervened. 'And behold', says 1 Kings 19:11, 'the LORD passed by, and a great and strong wind rent the mountains, and brake in pieces the rocks before the LORD; but the LORD was not in the wind: and after the wind an earthquake; but the LORD was not in the earthquake: and after the earthquake a fire; but the LORD was not in the fire: and after the fire a still small voice'. This was exactly what the prophet needed to hear deep down in his own heart.

And what a difference this voice made to him! It was tremendously refreshing. He was immediately enabled to get up and go, having 'wrapped his face in his mantle' (the Holy Spirit). Surely this is the sign of a true prophet. His natural characteristic features are covered over by the Holy Spirit, and they play no part in his ministry.

As we may have already seen hearing God's Word is not an automatic thing. It is no more automatic than serving Him. It is really a matter of choice. Joshua says "As for me and my house, we will serve the Lord." His mind was made up.

We have the ability to decide. This is an important, innate, God-given quality in everybody's life. In fact, we are almost unconsciously making decisions all the time, some of which have far reaching consequences for good or ill. For example, we have but to look at the book of Ruth. Here is a very interesting account of a man called Elimelech, with Naomi his wife, and their two sons Mahlon and Chilion.

The name Elimelech means 'my God is King'. As long as God was allowed to be King and to be directing this man's affairs all was well. The family was in a land that God had promised the children of Israel. Because of disobedience to God the whole nation had incurred punishment, there was a famine throughout the land. Nevertheless, God was looking after His people including Mr and Mrs Elimelech and family although they had to endure certain pressures.

It was at this point that the head of the Elimelech family with his wife made a decision which would completely change their life-style and circumstances. Having agreed that conditions must be better elsewhere they left their homeland for Moab. They had run out of patience, neglecting or deliberately forsaking God's promises. We likewise can often fail in this relation. Hebrews 6 tells us it is by faith and patience that we inherit the promises.

This was a decision that brought tragedy. They had

moved out to find an easier life, but it was in fact much harder. No sooner had they arrived in Moab than Elimelech died. That was the first sorrow. Soon after that Mahlon and Chilion married Moabitish women. That was the second sorrow as Moab was an idolatrous country, prosperous yes, but Godless.

Of the family, only Naomi was now left alive, together with her two daughters-in-law. It has been said that 'no man is an island'. How true that is! We need to act out the name 'Elimelech'. We need to acknowledge the Kingship of God in our individual lives. In our own natural thinking we are apt to try improving on God's provision and purpose for our lives and therefore face tragedy. To make matters worse the tragedy always involves others and what pain, what anguish of heart, there usually is. But for the one whose heart is tender toward God, and quick to repent over wrong decisions or choices made inadvisedly, He can turn the gloom into joy and the sadness into merriment.

Naomi had good news from her homeland 'that the Lord had visited His people in giving them bread'. She stirred herself — no doubt sorrowing over the error of judgement which had earned the present circumstances — she decided to return to Bethlehem-Judah. Her confession was "I went out full, and the Lord hath brought me home again empty."

The Lord can, and will always do something marvellous with an empty vessel. Whenever we turn to Him acknowledging our utter emptiness and desperate need of Him, He is sure to do something on our behalf. Incidentally, we see His operations regarding empty vessels in the account given in 2 Kings 4. Remember the widow being ministered to by the prophet Elijah?

He asked her to bring as many empty vessels as she could gather and to begin pouring into them from her little cruse of oil. She filled all of them. As long as she continued pouring, the oil flowed.

Does this not speak volumes to our hearts? The blessing of God makes rich and he adds no sorrow to it. This widow and her two sons entered into God's bounty. The prophet told her to sell the oil, pay off her debts, and live off the rest. No more poverty — good!

This is how God wants all of us to live — so linked into heaven's supplies that we never experience want (see Psalm 23).

Returning to Naomi's plight; we have to acknowledge that the will of God for us is always best, even though there might be the attendant pressures, oppositions and adversities. It is better to stay where God has put us rather than to move out to some other place where it looks easier or better.

Elimelech's sons were approaching marriageable age. We may well ask the question, why did he not think of that? For settling in a foreign land would almost automatically result in their taking wives from that country. But the pull of the world proved too strong for him, and so he emigrated supposing, we may suspect, that he could be excused for flouting God's laws as the times were so hard.

Many young people and even older ones seeking partners for marriage may do well to be warned by these examples in Scripture. God's Word says be not unequally yoked with unbelievers. In other words, God forbids that Christian should marry a non-Christian, or in any way be in partnership the one with the other. There can be no parleying with the world without severe consequences.

CHAPTER FIFTEEN

FROM DARKNESS INTO LIGHT

The only solution to be found is in Christ who sits and reigns from the throne. The new born babe in Christ cries out "Thy Kingdom come, Thy will be done." Now His will is all that matters.

The moment we are born again the Holy Spirit quickens our desire for Christ. We begin to long for Him to come and reign on the earth that His will may be done here as it is in heaven. If He is to be pre-eminent in our hearts, and in the Churches, there must be this radical change. Submission of our wills to His sovereign rule must be paramount. Should this not be the case, we are aligning ourselves with the Ephesian Church where the Lord had to say to the folk, you have lost your first love. The Lordship of Christ was not evident there.

So he said "Remember therefore from whence thou art fallen, and repent, and do the first works; or else I will come unto thee quickly, and will remove thy candlestick out of his place . . ." (Rev. 2:5). Sad to say that took place there.

The illuminating Divine presence went out of that place for one reason only. They had failed to maintain this indispensable principle. The Lordship of the Saviour was not acknowledged nor exercised in that church.

Another important question is this. How can this vital emphasis be maintained day by day, week by week, month by month and even year by year? How can we enjoy this priceless reality of Christ being in the midst of us? At Colosse the Christians were in similar difficulties. Paul writing to them outlines the need for the maintenance of this holy flame. He speaks of the "hope which is laid up for you in heaven." The stress here is on the Word of Truth of the Gospel.

In Colossians 1:23 he says 'Continue in the faith grounded and settled, and be not moved away from the hope of the Gospel, which ye have heard'. Make no mistake about this, the apostle was addressing himself to a people amongst whom there was a lack of continuity in spiritual stance. His burden was that Christ might be formed in them — that they might be living examples of the Gospel itself. So he introduced the one and only corrective; the proclamation of the Word of God. This uplifting of the Lord of Glory would place Him pre-eminently in the midst of His people.

The trouble was not the lack of preaching nor the lack of teaching. But human personalities had gained the ascendancy and so Christ diminished. Jesus was not Lord in that church. His presence and power were continually being undermined by human zeal, oratory and self-will. Paul's recommendation was singularly to restore and promote the testimony of Jesus Christ. This we see especially in the second chapter. In verse 8 he says 'beware lest any man spoil you . . .', in verse 16 'let no man therefore judge you . . .' and in verse 18 'let no man beguile you'.

There is only one foundation to which the Holy Ghost will always attest and it is this 'He (Christ) must increase, but I must decrease'. He must have all the glory. The human personality must give way and be utterly submerged beneath the Divine presence.

Could we not do with some straight talking in some of our churches today? Paul said "I, Brethren, when I came to you, came not with excellency of speech or of wisdom, declaring unto you the testimony of God. For I determined not to know anything among you, save Jesus Christ, and Him crucified. And I was with you in weakness, and in fear, and in much trembling. And my speech and my preaching was not with enticing words of man's wisdom, but in demonstration of the Spirit and of power: that your faith should not stand in the wisdom of men, but in the power of God."

This was not the expression of human timidity. Paul was a man of immense courage and boldness. From the time that Ananias had laid his hands upon him, shortly after his miraculous conversion, and the Holy Spirit had come upon him, he was God's man of faith and power. But something here at Colosse had overwhelmed his soul. The things that God had committed to him were so sacred, so precious, that he was fully persuaded they could not be subjected to defilement by human personality.

There is no place upon the entire face of the earth so sacred as where the Word of God is proclaimed. Conversely, there is no place so illfitting for the human personality as the pulpit. It is completely foreign and alien to this holy and precious exercise. This is what Paul had been saying to them. Is this not a thrilling responsibility? But, ah, so awesome and indeed so mighty.

Anyone who has not been overwhelmed with a sense of his own wretchedness, and unworthiness — anyone who has not been broken down and melted at the thought that his lips should publish this glorious truth to men and women everywhere is not qualified for this pursuit because of his lack of spiritual perception. Paul himself confessed this. He said "God forbid that I should glory, save in the cross of our Lord Jesus Christ, by whom the world is crucified unto me, and I unto the world."

What world? The world of praise, of human adoration and of fame. There is a prevalent, bogus, psychological method of bringing men and women into some kind of spiritual experience. This is often practised in mass campaigns or by the clever evangelist endeavouring to get people to make a decision to follow Christ. They go through certain formulae purporting to bring these unsuspecting folk into the Kingdom of God. This is obnoxious. It is also defiling to the whole testimony of the Truth and does much more harm than good.

Note what happened to Paul when he was smitten on the Damascus road. There was a light — a Divine awesome light which shone around him. What was that? The transforming glory of the Lord. This is still required today for people to be born into the Kingdom of God. There must be a communication, a shining, burning radiance from on high, slaying the individual and laying him prostrate at the feet of the Son of God.

Does not the Bible say 'the entrance of Thy words giveth light'? This must totally eclipse the darkness. 'This is the true Light, which lighteth every man that cometh into the world' according to John 1:9. Paul in his testimony said that light was above the brightness of the noonday sun. It transcended that of every natural source of illumination. He also heard a voice.

This was none other than the Lord's, imparting unto him His own nature in this inexplicable experience of the new birth.

If we are to see Divine success we must never be found trusting in our own methods or procedures. True faith can and will only operate upon the Divine statement. It is not our method, system, service or type of service which will promote the testimony of Jesus Christ. We stand upon what He says and the Holy Spirit will promote Him in every situation.

It is clear that Paul had never been to Colosse, but it was a place reputed for supernatural activity. Note he speaks of fruit in chapter one. 'For the hope which is laid up for you in heaven, whereof ye heard before in the Word of the truth of the Gospel; which is come unto you, as it is in all the world; and bringeth forth fruit, as it doth also in you, since the day ye heard of it, and knew the grace of God in truth'. It was by Divine activity that that fruit was brought forth. Verse 13 says 'who hath delivered us from the power of darkness, and hath translated us into the Kingdom of His dear Son'.

This is surely by Divine intervention that we are translated and this illustrates that every church should be a place of supernatural activity. It should also be a place of the confirmation of His truth in these precious operations of the grace of God in the hearts of men and women. There are two polarizations in the Church today. There are people who are so bent on the supernatural that nothing else seems to matter. They would have the supernatural demonstrated in every meeting. In a way nothing can honestly be said against all this, save that it borders on imbalance. We can have too much of one thing and too little of others.

Nevertheless, God does not put us in glass houses. There is a difference between His will and His providence. We ought not to suffer loss by being too cautious about extravagance. If the Word is continually being proclaimed in the midst of His people it will be correctly confirmed all the time by the Holy Spirit.

In the testimony of Acts 3 where we see the healing of the lame man these vital truths and principles are clear. The moment the transforming power of God came upon him he leaped up praising the Lord.

His focus was not now on Peter and John. He did not start campaigning for them, engineering ways or openings for their ministry, or giving any glowing account of them, which under the Divine scrutiny of the Holy Spirit would be of no value. God does not need our help for promoting the testimony of the Lord Jesus. About five thousand souls were born into the Kingdom that day, after 'many of them which heard the Word' — not from the miracle they had earlier witnessed.

How important it is to bear this principle in mind. The demonstration of the supernatural is not an end in itself. Any healing, any deliverance . . . does not become an end but is a pointer to the work of God advancing the testimony of Jesus Christ. He said "now you are clean through the Word which I have spoken unto you." The application of the Word of God always purifies the individual or Church. Sad to say this is the ministry which is not very popular in our day in many of our Churches.

There are many in great adversity simply because the ministers will not stand up and faithfully deliver or use the Sword of the Spirit. They will not apply the searching, delivering truth. In the days of Ezekiel God looked down from heaven saying, 'I sought for a man among them, that should make up the hedge, and stand in the gap before me for the land, that I should not destroy it: but I found none. Therefore have I poured out mine indignation upon them . . . .' (Ezek. 22:30,31).

If God was looking for a man then, prior to Jesus' coming, 'full of grace and truth', being 'the mediator of a better covenant, which was established upon better promises', He is certainly now looking for men. He is seeking elders, ministers, and everyone who will stand up and be counted for Christ's sake. Remember Revelation? Christ exposed the situation in everyone of those places. He said you must do the first works. You must repent or your candlestick will be removed. I know all about your good works, but . . . .

It is doubtful whether there has ever been a time when good works were more popular in churches than in our day — missionary endeavour, youth clubs, care for the poor, sheltering the homeless . . . . The Lord sees all these things, but He is calling unto us that we gather in the house of the Lord and really cry unto Him.

What shall we cry? 'Revive Thy work, O Lord'. He will thoroughly purge His threshing floor. This is the Divine process. He is looking for men to reap with Him the wheat and the barley. From thence we may progress to the vineyard. But note that something remarkable has taken place. 'The vine is dried up . . .' according to Joel 1:12. The '. . . new vine is dried up . . . .' (verse 10).

For our service to be successful in the Lord there must be this indispensable emphasis on the restoration of the vine, both old and new. They must thrive and indeed flourish. Their being dried up, you may also note, was not through lack of rain. Joel 1:4 typifies the march of an army upon the Church leaving her desolate. The entire chapter is a picture of gloom, speaking to us of a great spiritual dearth, a tragic absence of the wine of the Holy Spirit. So great is the devastation that if that were all that this prophet had to say there would be no hope for us. "The field is wasted, the land mourneth; for the corn is wasted: the new wine is dried up, the oil languisheth . . . because joy is withered away from the sons of men."

Despite all this, there is a promise from God associated with 'the remnant whom the Lord shall call'. God has given His Word that there will come a time of deliverance. 'I will restore to you the years that the locust hath eaten . . . .'

But this is not going to take place automatically. On our part there must be a genuine turning to the Lord. His people must seek Him, humbly repenting before Him, owning our desperate failure to receive and proclaim with Holy zeal the Sword of the Spirit. We must 'Howl and lament . . .' in true penitence. 'Therefore also now, saith the Lord, turn ye even to me with all your heart, and with fasting, and with weeping, and with mourning: and rend your heart, and not your garments . . .' (Joel 2:12,13).

Heart-rending though this demand is, it is neither crushing nor irksome. Backed by that sure promise of God (Joel 2:28) it is shortly to be realized when He shall pour out His Spirit upon all flesh. What a time of prosperity that will be when our affections shall be entirely focussed on the One who is the solution to every situation. In the meantime what better thing can we do than wait upon Him. May this be ever our continual desire that Christ may be pre-eminent.

CHAPTER SIXTEEN

THE NEW MAN

Waiting upon the Lord does not necessarily mean sitting down allowing time, as it were, to pass by. If ever I go into a restaurant or hotel I have great pleasure in being waited on by some polite waiter or waitress, one who is interested in me as a client. I always feel good about it, it is never any problem for me to tip that person well, and I always look forward to returning to such a place should the occasion arise. This illustration is a bird's eye view of how gratifying it must be to God when we serve Him with gladness, reading His Word, praying, making intercession and giving thanks unto His Holy name.

We may also draw 'joy' from the wells of salvation. Where are they? Inside of us. We do not have to see them to believe that they are there any more than we have to see our liver or spleen to believe that they are inside of us. As we believe so by faith we draw from these wells. The more we draw the greater the flow. We simply experience Ephesians chapter 4 all over again by 'being filled with the Holy Spirit'. This is one of the things the Church needs today. Jesus said He that believeth in Me out of his innermost being shall flow rivers of living water. There is an abundance of Holy Spirit material inside just waiting to be manifested for the glory of God.

I have not slept in church for many years, at least not since the Holy Spirit quickened me. He completely cured me of that. This should not be surprising when we realize that the Bible says "if the Spirit of Him who raised Jesus from the dead dwells within you, then the God who raised Christ Jesus from the dead will also give new life to your mortal bodies through His indwelling Spirit" (Rom. 8:11, N.E.B.).

The trouble with me was that I did not know that God has a programme. Going to church then was just a duty, whereas He wanted me to be so filled with Himself that I might overflow. What does this mean? It was never God's intention that His people should be self-contained. We are born again to reproduce. Here is a very important point symbolized in Scripture from as early as Genesis 49:22. 'Joseph is a fruitful bough, even a fruitful bough by a wall; whose branches run over the wall.' This is tremendous, signifying as it does that we are destined to be channels of blessing. We see something of this same principle expressed in Psalm 23:5, 'Thou anointest my head with oil; my cup runneth over'.

Essentially the anointing is concerned with priestly service. God's love which, according to the Scriptures, is shed abroad in our hearts by the Holy Spirit must overflow — must reach others — must spread His light and nature to humanity through human channels which are made ready for this purpose.

For humanity to serve God our bodies in which we once served sin must be covered over by nothing less than a heaven sent garment. Consider Elijah and Elisha for instance. The latter received the mantle that fell to him from Elijah who himself had been taken up into heaven. God's plan for His Church today is that individually we must be mantled with the power of Another. That power must come from above downwards, enveloping and separating us for the promotion of our Master's interests. This all transcending power-packed garment must be in evidence — must be paramount; giving the super-ability not only to do, but to endure.

Look at Moses. How did he become useful to God? The Bible says he 'was learned in all the wisdom of the Egyptians and was mighty in words and in deeds' (Acts 7:22). That was fine, but to what end?

During his prime as Prince of Egypt that country was the centre of the then known world. People everywhere were looking to Egypt as the trend setter in fashions, industry, commerce, education — in all the earthly possessions which on a purely natural level are supposed to make life worthwhile. In the spiritual sense then, Egypt in Scripture means the world. Moses was at the very head of that world. He was answerable to no one in all the earth but Pharaoh the King. What a tremendous contrast to the man that he would eventually be.

Some of us might be tempted to think that this Moses would be of tremendous worth in the Church. But God did not use him as he was. Despite his brilliant education, his eloquence, regal status, wealth and power he was totally unsuitable. He had to be fashioned by the Holy Spirit, broken, moulded and fitted for a heaven centred life of adventure. By the time he was to take charge of God's people to lead them out of Egypt he was a new man with new and different motives. 'That which is born of the flesh is flesh; and that which is born of the Spirit is Spirit' (John 3:6).

There is a saying that 'life begins at forty'. Essentially this was so for Moses. He was fully that age when it came into his heart to visit his brethren, the children of Israel. The Bible does not say he had a revelation from heaven. It does not say the Holy Spirit led him, but it is evident that somehow Moses began to believe he would be God's choice for delivering his suffering people from slavery under Pharaoh. Was his perception right? Was his timing right? God is never in a hurry.

One day Moses saw an Egyptian slave driver harassing one of the slaves. Thinking this was a fine opportunity to commence his deliverance ministry, Moses sprang into action. He looked this way and that, according to the Bible, then he killed the Egyptian and buried him in the sand.

What a difference it would have made had he looked to the Lord? Most, if not all of us tend to behave like Moses, looking around us for help when we are confronted with making certain decisions. We may rely on the help of people or even circumstances. At best these will only end in disappointment. The Bible warns that the arm of flesh will fail us.

Moses thought no one had seen him murder that man. The next day he tried to part two Israelites who were fighting, and had the shock of his life as one of them turned to him and asked whether he would kill him as he had the Egyptian on the previous day.

'My . . .!' thought Moses. 'How on earth did he find this out? The next thing will be that Pharaoh will be having my head off'. And so he fled the country to Midian, to the 'backside of the desert', according to the Bible.

A man with the Spirit of God upon him, does not

have to behave like this. He does not have to run away from anybody or anything. The Scripture says 'the righteous are bold as a lion'. It is when we are out of God's will that cowardice and fear of the enemy assail us.

We cannot serve God in the flesh. His Word to us is clear. 'If ye live after the flesh, ye shall die: but if ye through the Spirit do mortify the deeds of the body, ye shall live'.

Acting in the flesh Moses nearly lost his own life. Here now in a foreign country this Prince of the Realm of Egypt was to be exposed to the rigours and hardships that would be nothing but medicine to his soul.

As we consider Moses' trials and testings it is comforting to remember that God will never suffer any of us to be tested or tried above that which we are able to bear. 'He knoweth our frame; He remembereth that we are dust'. When the pressure is on we can be sure that something good is happening, even as David said "O God of my righteousness: Thou hast enlarged me when I was in distress."

The righteousness of Moses' God had to be manifested in every area of his life, despite the painful process. That murderous nature had to give place to that loving, caring compassionate spirit of the Lord. As we have said it would take time, but that was not important. What was most important was that it would cost Moses everything, the whole of his old way of life. Forty years hence he was destined to emerge with heavenly vision, courage, boldness, ability and infinitely higher goals. God's ways are certainly not our ways. In order that Moses might become a shepherd to the Israelites he had to take care of sheep.

It was from this low estate and training that the title 'Prince of Egypt' would pale into insignificance in the light of that which God had prepared for him, even Moses 'the man of God' (Deut 33:1). Often earthly titles are coveted as invaluable status symbols, but in the final analysis, are they really? At best they are but transient. But Moses' title is for ever enshrined in God's Holy Word.

In a certain sense it took Moses forty years even to see clearly. While tending sheep in the wilderness he saw a bush on fire. This was a very special sight, one that God would have us all by the Spirit to behold, a burning bush that is never consumed. What was the significance of this but an ordinary man aflame with God? Is this not what the Lord does with us? The wealth of His Divine power is ever being poured out into us as we are pouring out unto others. Up to this time Moses as he stood had not received either the authority or the ability to be God's man.

It is easy to covet, being like the new Moses, as we read of him having power with God and over hosts of people, leading them out of captivity and through the wilderness. But wait a minute. Let us consider the cost. It is not cheap. It will cost us everything, our very lives — a life for a life — ours for Jesus'.

To be broken by the Holy Spirit is not irksome, except to the flesh, which He is for ever striving to replace with Christlikeness. God does not hurt anyone. The Bible says 'Thy people shall be willing in the day of Thy power'. He gives us a new and willing heart to be in tune with heaven. The Scriptures liken His perfecting us to wine preserving. Men do not 'put new wine into old bottles: else the bottles break, and the wine runneth out, and the bottles perish: but they put

new wine into new bottles, and both are preserved'
(Matt. 9:17).

Many good and faithful Christians in the sense that
we have been discussing are not usable. They are
faithful, but ineffective. Their lives are changed in
that they have received forgiveness of their sins, and
they pay their dues on every hand. Yet, spiritually they
do not progress. Moses had to arrive at a place in his
life where he could take and act upon instructions
from heaven. Worldly wisdom plays no part in
heavenly matters.

The very best thing that we can do is die, as Jesus
shows us in John 12:24 'Except a corn of wheat fall into
the ground and die, it abideth alone: but if it die, it
bringeth forth much fruit'. Only the Holy Spirit can
effect this precious fruit-bearing change in our lives as
we yield to Him. Hence Jesus said further "he that
loveth his life shall lose it; and he that hateth his life in
this world shall keep it unto life eternal."

Of course, this was signifying His own death and
resurrection that would take place on Calvary for sin.
It is recorded in Luke 9:51 that Jesus 'stedfastly set
His face to go to Jerusalem'. What better example of
earnest desire to accomplish the will of Another could
there have been? Wholly dependent, He journeyed
irrevocably toward Calvary.

It would be foolish to imagine that Jesus did not
know what He was about to face in the Garden of
Gethsemane; the terrible shame, suffering, condemnation and eventual death (Mark 13:36; Luke 22:42).

He received power from on high to lay down His life
and to take it up again. Angelic hosts were standing by
ready to rescue Him from this terrible plight, but He
was unflinching in His determination to do His

Father's will. He died alone, the just for the unjust to bring us to God. Let us never forget that God always equips us for every situation into which He allows us to come. He will even cause us to go through fire and water if that is what it will take to produce the life of Christ in us.

In this process there might be sorrow, there might be pain. How can there be brokenness without some degree of suffering? We may be encouraged as we listen to what Paul says about this matter, 'For I reckon that the sufferings of this present time are not worthy to be compared with the glory which shall be revealed in us' (Rom. 8:18). He obviously kept his eye of faith on God's plan for His people and was better qualified than most of us will ever be to talk of suffering for Christ's sake.

Let us take another look at some of the difficulties he had. He had hardly received salvation before the Jews began plotting to kill him (Acts 9:23). In Acts 9:26 we find that he was hindered from joining the disciples at Jerusalem. But for Barnabas who took pity on him and defended him before the apostles it appears he would never have been accepted among them.

The catalogue goes on. Acts 13:6-13 shows how Satan opposed him. Verses 44-49 declare how he was opposed by the Jewish people; and in verses 50-52 we are told that both he and Barnabas were expelled, as undesirables, from Antioch in Pisidia.

Wherever Paul went he was sure to be in some trouble or other. He and Barnabas were no sooner away from Antioch than they were on their way to Iconium where they were soon mobbed (Acts 14:1-5). Then fleeing to Lystra and Derbe they were stoned,

Paul being left for dead (Acts 14:6-19). In addition to all these things he had the perils of continually disputing with false brethren (Acts 19:8). At Philippi, (Acts 16:10-40) he was beaten and jailed. At Thessalonica (Acts 17:1-10) he was mobbed and expelled. The same happened to him at Berea (Acts 17:10-14), at Corinth, (Acts 18:1-23) and at Ephesus (Acts 19:23-41). There was another plot against his life by the Jews (Acts 20:3).

This list of his hardships — seized, tried in court, imprisoned, beaten, and later on even shipwrecked — though possibly horrifying to some of us today is not in any sense exhaustive.

How do our apparently hard times measure up to Paul's? It is particularly encouraging as we read his testimony to find that he always attributed his stamina to Christ being his goal, also the ministry which he received from Him. No wonder he was so positive in all his talk, and all that he said was backed by action. 'And now, behold, I go bound in the spirit unto Jerusalem, not knowing the things that shall befall me there:' he said (Acts 20:22). This was not the language of fright or fear, but of confidence that his whole life was safely in the hands of Another.

H

CHAPTER SEVENTEEN

BORDER CHRISTIANS

There is no evidence in Scripture that Paul ever lost his confidence. He was always buoyant. In everything he saw himself as triumphant, keeping his eye of faith on the victory of the Cross of Christ.

There could hardly have been a more difficult place than Corinth for the preaching of the Gospel. Yet, here was Paul, God's man on the spot, witnessing for his Saviour, as strongly as at any other place. He lived, worked and taught here for nearly two years. Apart from the time he spent at Ephesus this was his longest stay in any city. Might this not be that he deliberately chose to remain so long in this area to demonstrate the ability in the Holy Spirit to overcome adversity? When like him we can with a true heart say 'the world is crucified unto me, and I unto the world' then and only then shall we really prove that 'we are more than conquerors through Him that loved us'.

Paul's only boast was Christ. The self-life never got in the way to rob him of his spiritual progress. It is not possible to overstress the dangers of putting oneself forward.

A true witness unto Jesus will only testify of Him, leaving no room for self. Whatever the Holy Spirit does through us never attracts any glory to ourselves. His is

114

the power, the might, the authority and the glory.

By his ministry at Corinth Paul showed the Divine power and effectiveness that belongs to all overcomers. He demonstrated quite clearly that there is a way for all men to rise from being sinners to saints. Listen to the authority with which he speaks, the Spirit of the Almighty being in charge. Do you not know 'that the unrighteous shall not inherit the kingdom of God?' Be not deceived: neither the immoral, nor idolaters, adulterers, homosexuals, thieves, the greedy, drunkards, revilers, robbers will inherit the Kingdom of God — 'and such were some of you' (1Cor. 6:9-11).

Does this sound like a man who is timid and retiring? The Bible says 'the fear of man bringeth a snare'. In other words if we are afraid of men our witness unto Jesus will never be effective. Generally speaking, men would trap us, seeking every conceivable opportunity to frustrate our witness unto Christ. Divine boldness, however, is not subject to men's snares. This is pointedly emphasised in Luke 10:19 'Behold, I give unto you power to tread on serpents and scorpions, and over all the power of the enemy: and nothing shall by any means hurt you'. What Jesus has said here can easily be put another way and retain the same meaning. Nobody through whom the enemy is working shall ever overcome you, making you feel ashamed, hurt or frustrated. You will always be in a position to prove yourself victorious.

Remember Jesus cleansing the temple? If ever there was a place full of enemies that was it. But the record shows that He was utterly fearless, and was totally successful in what He had set out to accomplish. He knew that He had the authority for He was not doing His own will but His Father's. This was in effect a *carte blanche* approval by God to do whatever was in the interest of His own house. Hence the Scriptures say '. . . you have granted Him power and authority over all flesh' (Amp. Bible John 17:2).

Note no one ever questioned Jesus' ability, but His authority presented a real challenge. It was now manifest to all that there was something at the back of this Man's life, something more than could be understood by the natural man. It follows then that if everybody is understanding us there is something wrong with our lives. Who can understand the ways of the Lord? 'How unsearchable are His judgments, and His ways past finding out' says Romans 11:33. Is not this one of the reasons why He said 'Woe unto you, when all men shall speak well of you'?

Some people criticized Him, others mocked Him; and there were always plots against His life, or to drive Him out of towns and places. He remained, however, a man amongst men.

Why did so many leave their occupations to follow Him? They left their homes, they left their families, their livelihoods and everything else. At His command fevers abated, sicknesses relented, devils fled and even the winds and the weather obeyed Him, all because of His irresistible authority as He persisted in testifying not of Himself but of His Father who had sent Him.

The secret of His incomparable success was that He was a man under authority. He was the Sent One. How often He alluded to this! 'My meat' said He, 'is to do the will of Him that sent me, and to finish His work' (John 4:34). 'He that honoureth not the Son honoureth not the Father which hath sent Him' (John 5:23). 'I can of mine own self do nothing: as I hear, I judge: and my judgement is just; because I seek not mine own will, but the will of the Father which hath sent me' (John 5:30).

Perhaps this is where many of us are failing. Our spiritual lives are a shambles because we are not ourselves under authority, and the enemy of our souls is aware of this. Be assured, he will not miss the slightest opportunity of taking advantage of such a situation. In Luke 7 the centurion whom we discussed on page 48 asked Jesus to come and heal his servant who was at the point of dying. Jesus started on His way to visit the servant with a view to granting the request. And when he was near the house the centurion sent again, but this time the request was a little different. He told the Lord not to bother to call at the house as he did not feel worthy for Him to enter under his roof, nor to actually face Him. But, said he unto the Lord, 'say in a word, and my servant shall be healed'.

This was tremendous! Our Fellowships and Churches could really profit by having a few members like this man. And we could do with being like him. Listen to this! 'For I also am a man set under authority', he said, 'having under me soldiers, and I say unto one, Go, and he goeth; and to another Come, and he cometh; and to my servant, Do this, and he doeth it'. What the centurion was saying was that he discerned the total effectiveness of Jesus' words, for as far as he was concerned they were not really His, but those of a Higher Power which was infallible. And that Jesus' being subject to that Power, anything that He said would come to pass.

Here was a man seeing things as they really were. It is not recorded that he was even a lover or follower of Jesus. One or two things are clear about him, though. He was a man of great faith, as Jesus said, and he could see the difference between the self-life and that of One who is under authority being sent by Another. He knew and respected the power that resulted from this delegated authority. It is particularly interesting that when John the Baptist was testifying of Jesus he was asked to say who he was, and he did not even give his name. All he said of himself was that he was simply 'a voice crying in the wilderness'.

If there were any room for self, the Early Church as detailed in Acts would have been full of it. They might have had something of which to boast; the signs, the wonders, the miracles, the healings that were daily manifested among them were enough to turn their heads. But as it was, the Holy Spirit was in charge and the Church never claimed to be the custodian of the power or the authority that motivated it. All the Christians were only witnesses unto the person of the risen Lord. Significantly, His name is used so very often in Acts. If we seek to promote ourselves we shall have an unhappy life and even destruction at the end like Judas Iscariot. So Jesus warns us 'take heed, and beware of covetousness: for a man's life consisteth not in the abundance of things which he possesseth'.

How might we identify this self-life? It is really the uncommitted carnal nature. The converse is the spiritual life. The spiritual man is the very opposite to Lot, that Old Testament character whose life-style and tragic end stand out like a beacon — a danger signal for all to see.

The spiritual man will not strive. He commits his life to God. Abraham said, Lot we must not strive 'for we be brethren . . . . If thou wilt take the left hand, then I will go to the right; or if thou depart to the right hand, then I will go to the left' (Gen. 13:9).

We may think Lot might have said, no, Uncle Abraham, it cannot be right for me to just have my own way, like this seeing how much you have given me and indeed cared for me all these years. But no, he was not even a little embarrassed. The carnal man will fight for his rights, and what is more, he will not relent until he gets them. Lot got all he wanted. He looked toward Sodom and Gomorrah — the well-watered plains. What he did not realize was that sin was down there, and he was soon to be found settled by Jordan, right on the border of those wicked cities.

We cannot afford to parley with wickedness. There is a proverb that says 'if we play with fire, we shall get burnt'. Being on the border of sin is always a risky business. The apostle Paul tells us what happens to that which touches anything that is unclean, it becomes unclean itself.

We do not have to be very imaginative to perceive what happened to Lot. It was not long before he was finding his way over into Sodom and Gomorrah, identifying himself with local customs, language and everything else.

As we saw in an earlier chapter Jesus taught us to pray 'lead us not into temptation, but deliver us from evil'. Might we expect this deliverance if we, like Lot, deliberately expose ourselves so blatantly to sin and fall therein?

Soon Lot was so unified with the people of those lands that he even became a judge in the city sitting in the gates. Obviously he had to 'hide his light under a bushel'. The grabbing spirit of this world was at work in this man. God save us from this way of living. 'Love not the world, neither the things that are in the world' says 1 John 2:15. Who can deny that it is good to have a worthwhile position in the world, but there is something far more important than that for us. How can we ever sacrifice the way of righteousness for any earthly position or possession? Regarding himself as no more than a steward of anything that he had in this world, Abraham kept a loose hold on things. Note from these verses in Genesis 13 that he determined to lay down everything for the sake of peace.

His advice to his nephew to choose wherever he would like to settle was not the result of a hasty decision. Nor was Abraham grudgingly putting an end to a quarrel that he had not started. When we are sure of our place in God we can afford to let the carnal man have his way. In the end he will be the loser.

The Bible says 'the way of the transgressor is hard'. God has shown us the Way. 'This book of the law (the Bible) shall not depart out of thy mouth; but thou shalt meditate therein day and night,' is His Word to us, 'that thou mayest observe to do according to all that is written therein: for then thou shalt make thy way prosperous, and then thou shalt have good success' (Josh. 1:8). In this short passage two particular points are well worth underlining. The total responsibility for prosperity is presented as being in our own hands. The way we choose to live is all important. If the Word of God is our only guide our way of life will automatically be prosperous. This is what is emphasized here as point one.

Point two is concerned with the type of success. Our text speaks of the 'good' type which presupposes that there is also a 'bad'. So in a certain sense it is really up to us to make our own choice. Lot very definitely chose his. We shall come back to this again.

God's Word does not only declare the basis for

success in the realm of finance. It states the actual purpose for the success. Hear what Paul says in his teaching about generosity. 'And God is able to make all grace abound toward you; that ye, always having all sufficiency in all things, may abound to every good work. As it is written, He hath dispersed abroad; He hath given to the poor: his righteousness remaineth for ever . . . . Being enriched in every thing to all bountifulness, which causeth through us thanksgiving to God' (2 Cor. 9:8-11).

No doubt Lot's life-style, if sought out, can be found in many of our churches and fellowships today. He is typical of a Christian who is off course, not caring very much about spiritual matters. Has it ever struck you that we are not told what his wife's name was, nor the names of his daughters or sons-in-law. We are cautioned, however, 'remember Lot's wife!' Why? If we recalled no more than her death we shall have had a tremendous insight into the climax of a life lived outside of God. Leaving the details of the family life for a moment the next thing is that neither Lot nor any of that entire household recognized the voice of Divine intervention. When the angels came to Sodom and Gomorrah announcing imminent destruction planned by God, they did not even know that they were angels. But when they called on Abraham he knew who they were. And note how duly respectful he was in addressing them — 'my Lord'.

Christianity being a wholly separate matter, this is to say we are separated unto God and experientially living in His presence, we quite naturally like Abraham know His voice.

This brings out the point of communion. In 1 Corinthians 10 this is discussed. When you go into a place, eat what is set before you, says the text. Paul asks what fellowship has this with the table of demons. The Holy Spirit being the Spirit of Truth the Scriptures are understood in the light that He sheds on them. What we understand here is that in no way could Lot have recognized the angels because he was not communing with God's people but with the world. For a time he was no more than a border Christian, as we chose to call him, but at this particular point he was not even that. He had capitulated to the enemy, as far as his testimony to Christ on earth was concerned. How much a warning this should be to all of us!

We need to get away from the border into where the blessing of God is really flowing freely. Remember the story of Zicklag as detailed in 1 Samuel 30:1-4 how it was attacked, how it was ravaged. Look into this. Study the aftermath. You will find it was borderland. Our place in the Father's Kingdom is to be in the centre of His will, communing with Him and His people.

CHAPTER EIGHTEEN

THE SPIRITUAL BATTLE

Some people hate quiet. It is doubtful whether there were many quiet places in Sodom or Gomorrah. The hubbub must have been outrageous, at least God had evidently come to the conclusion that it was. What with the self-gratification, the perversion, the flirtation, the obscenity and many other 'pleasures of sin' which abounded; it was plain debauchery.

We must not think these people were not cultured. They certainly were, but the higher, and the more sophisticated the culture, the less the spirituality. In fact, this was the trouble. These people did not give thanks to God for anything. He was never in their thoughts. Their land was the type of place in which we as Christians would not choose to settle, save to preach the Gospel.

A prolonged spate of Holy Ghost silence before the Lord is anybody's best medicine. It reveals our inner state, giving us an opportunity of putting matters right with the Lord. 'Be still, and know that I am God' says the Bible. 'In quietness and in confidence shall be your strength'.

Some people squirm as they are being penetrated by the Divine radiance that is peculiar to such quiet, the presence of the Lord can be so potent, so deeply searching. We may suspect that Mr and Mrs Lot and the family knew nothing of this glorious state of being. It is not without significance that the angels had to practically drag them out of the city. Lot was so weary, so spiritually lethargic that they even had to speak harshly to him, in order that he should hurriedly escape to the mountains.

But, said Lot on the way, let me stay in this little city. Do not weary me by sending me far away. It is important for us to realize that but for Abraham, none of these would have escaped the holocaust. And why did Lot's wife look back? Because all her possessions, her ambitions, affections and aspirations lay in those evil cities which were under God's judgement.

Let a man count the cost, and denying himself every self-interest, be committed to the Almighty. Let his committment be pure and simple and his faith will sustain him. The people who scheme and sacrifice to make a name for themselves, wishing to be great in this world; what are they going to do in the end? Where are they going? Will their ego profit them anything? There will be many tears shed, but uselessly, in the shortly coming day, by people who should know and do better.

While the time is still available to us we ought really to take refuge in the Lord. This is the message that the Holy Spirit is bringing to our hearts right now. Lot lost everything for which he had striven, and in the end his very life was in the balance.

The Bible leaves us in no doubt as to how we may securely build our lives, for the wise Master Builder has already laid the foundation, according to 1 Corinthians 3:10-15. We are warned 'But let every man take heed how he buildeth thereupon. For other foundation can no man lay than that is laid, which is Jesus Christ. Now if any man build upon this foundation gold, silver, precious stones, wood, hay, stubble; every man's work shall be made manifest: for the day shall declare it . . . If any man's work shall be burned, he shall suffer loss: but he himself shall be saved; yet so as by fire'.

This is the challenge of the moment. What are we building? And what materials are we using? The gold typifying God, silver Jesus, and precious stones the Holy Spirit, will obviously come through the fire. But what of the wood, hay, and stubble — the rubbish, the easily ignitable? How shall they fare?

Lot evidently survived the test, only just, but nothing of his building did. All those years that he had spent acquiring wealth, fame, notoriety; wasted. Time is inestimably precious, and there is no way of recapturing it once it has gone. 'For our God is a consuming fire' (Heb. 12:29).

None of us shall receive any commendation or reward from our Heavenly Father for any building that is not praiseworthy. Worldly acquisitions, attainments and aspirations shall pass away. For none of these things shall we ever hear the promised 'well done, thou good and faithful servant . . . .'

Remember Peter recounting 'Lot, vexed with the filthy conversation of the wicked: (for that righteous man dwelling among them, in seeing and hearing, vexed his righteous soul from day to day with their unlawful deeds)' (2 Peter 2:7,8). God is merciful. When we analyze Lot's rescue that He performed we cannot help being amazed. But let us not forget that in every event of our compromise or complacency others are either directly or indirectly involved with us.

In an earlier chapter we touched on this by

illustrating that no man is an island. This is true all through life. Many people are wounded, some even fatally, by the sheer selfishness, greed or lack of consideration from others.

It was not only Lot's wife who perished. His sons-in-law also did. And in the very special circumstances in which they were, who is to tell whether many of those cities might not have turned to God in repentance, had Lot's life-style and witness been otherwise.

As for his daughters, who in fact only just managed to escape with him through the insistence of the angels, consider what happened to them. This was possibly the worst disgrace that had ever taken place in the history of Israel. Their deliberate incestuous conspiracy involving their father was of immense moral import.

Note from the record in Genesis 19 that it was not an inordinate desire for sexual fulfillment that made them commit this great wickedness. It was because they had no faith. 'Come,' said the one to the other, 'let us make our father drink wine, and we will lie with him, that we may preserve seed of our father'.

No doubt the desire of these young women was inborn. They had said in other words, let us protect our power, our honour in this world. We must produce children to carry on after us. They were not in the least concerned about what God thought of this matter.

This was clearly a case of sowing and reaping. 'Be not deceived' says the Bible. 'God is not mocked: for whatsoever a man soweth, that shall he also reap. For he that soweth to his flesh shall of the flesh reap corruption; but he that soweth to the Spirit shall of the Spirit reap life everlasting' (Gal. 6:7,8).

The Holy Spirit being our Blessed Comforter, He

delights in promoting those interests which always serve us best. Many of the conflicts through which we pass daily may be avoided. If only we could all clearly see that the spirit of the world is constantly at war with us, and not persons, circumstances, conditions and the like, how much better off we would be. We would do well to 'stand still, and see the salvation of the Lord.'

'Speak ye comfortably to Jerusalem, and cry unto her, that her warfare is accomplished . . . .' says Isaiah 40:2. According to this all we have to do is rest in the Lord.

CHAPTER NINETEEN

THE VICTORY

How might we recognize a person who is separated from the world and in tune with his Maker? In ourselves we have no criterion for this — and, what is more — it is hardly our business. But let us not forget that to the spiritual nothing is hidden.

There are a few general rules which are infallible. A genuinely close walk with the Lord is never in vain. When we are entirely given over to Him one thing is certain, we do not go about unnoticed. Whether consciously or unconsciously, for one reason or another, all eyes are on us. Some are bound to look on critically. But for the grace of God some of us may resent this. We may even feel tempted to be sorry for being so different from others who are embarrassed by our Christian principles. This is dangerous, as it could lead us into compromise.

The world will not in the end thank us for being unfaithful. They expect our standards to be high. They know instinctively that there is a division between us and themselves. But if we stoop, and it would have to be a stoop, to their level even for a moment we are in fact doing them a grave disservice. They will automatically conclude that we have nothing better than they already possess, as it was in the case of this minister whom a friend of mine encountered. He should have been representing the Gospel. But was he?

Calling at the offices of a particular organization in town my friend wanted to see this clergyman who was chaplain to the workers there. At the reception desk a man greeted him and asked what help he needed. "I would like to have a word with Rev . . . . ., is he available please?" asked my friend.

"I will get him for you in just a few minutes. Can you wait? I must not disturb him for the moment as he is downstairs having a drink with the boys." As he was offered a seat in the waiting room the polite receptionist continued talking with him, and my friend asked him what kind of man was the clergyman.

"Well," said he, "you could not wish for a better chaplain in a busy place like this. He never bothers us with religion. You will never find him bringing that sort of thing into conversation to embarrass us. Of course, he curses and swears like any of us and is always good for a joke, and a laugh with the boys. You should see him when we have a dance . . . I reckon he is a jolly good fellow."

Horrified, my friend tried desperately to change the conversation into something more wholesome, but the man rushed out, and soon came back ushering in Rev. . . . who was unsteady on his feet and unclear in his speech. Was not that minister's behaviour a travesty of anything that even remotely relates to the name of the Lord? Let us be warned lest any of us be found to be as the blind leading the blind.

There are those too, whose eyes may be upon us for praise. They will try to make us feel very important. Many do not find fault with this, as it appeals to their ego; but here again there is an underlying danger. The

J

moment we begin to enjoy any earthly adulation or approval our spiritual ears will suffer, and our progress will be halted. This is why Jesus warns 'woe unto you, when all men shall speak well of you'.

Some will admire us simply for what they think they can get out of us. These can be, and often are, a drain on our spiritual energy, a virtual waste of time. They usually engage our attention under the pretext that they badly need to talk with someone. We may take great care in talking with them quite interestedly only to discover later that it was not worth it. The time involved might have been much better spent doing something else. May God ever keep us from being deceived.

It is particularly noticeable that outward pressure did not alter the faithfulness of the saints of the early Church. It rather illustrated the Divine workmanship — the new creation. It showed to the world that ordinary human beings in whom the Lord was alive and doing well were invincible. It also made clear the fact that those men of God were able to stand up to pressure and not surrender the Truth. How gratifying it must have been to Christ to see His own Spirit on display! Those men were in the world but not of it.

It is fascinating to read of Paul and the authority which he wielded over the spirit of the world. The difference between a man like that and some of us is that he knew the enemy's tactics well, and never failed to demonstrate his victory over them in Christ's name.

In Exodus 17 we read that 'the LORD will have war with Amalek from generation to generation'. We, like the children of Israel, have been delivered from Egypt and Pharaoh's bondage. That in itself is a tremendous miracle. But what is the purpose of it? That we might be separated unto God for a wonderful life of praise, worship, adoration and witness.

When we gather together as a church or fellowship in His name it is always in view of finality. It is a life-style over which the Holy Spirit is presiding, as we are preparing for our eternal abode. This will culminate in a final gathering when we 'shall be caught up together . . . to meet the Lord in the air'.

In the meantime the fact that we have to separate one from another and go to our several homes is just a reminder that we are still in our bodies of humiliation, but the desire is continually with us to come together. What could quite justifiably be said of us is that we are having several rehearsals for our ascent to heaven.

We are destined to be skilled in the Word of righteousness. We develop this way on account of habit. Our meetings are just this, habitual, but how precious! The Bible speaks of full grown men, who on account of 'use have their senses exercised to discern both good and evil' (see Hebrews 5:14).

But it is not going to be paradise, not yet. That is for later on. For the time being there will be warfare. We shall be under attack from the enemy. There does not need to be any panic though, for we have the blessed assurance that the battle is not ours to fight. It is the Lord's. We are His property, and He is our defence, our strong tower, our fortress.

This warfare is clearly illustrated in this chapter of Exodus. 'Then came Amalek, and fought with Israel in Rephidim,' says verse 8. Looking into the details of the story we find that Amalek struck just after the smiting of the rock at Horeb. The apostle Paul takes up this incident and in writing to the Corinthians he assured them that 'that Rock was Christ' (1 Cor. 10:4). It was on our behalf that He was smitten at Calvary where from His side flowed blood and water.

Had Jesus' blood not been shed our sins would never have been remitted. So the blood speaks to us of His redeeming work, while the water, of the outpouring of the Holy Spirit on the day of Pentecost.

Who is Amalek? He is that subtle enemy, the flesh. Galatians 5:17 helps here. 'For the flesh lusteth against the Spirit, and the Spirit against the flesh: and these are contrary the one to the other'.

We must understand that the warfare is continuous. It started as soon as we were born again. Note from verse 8 once more 'then came Amalek'. There is no indication that he is ever intending to leave. He has come to stay. It is a day-long battle 'until the going down of the sun'. When Joshua led Israel, Amalek attacked them, and under King Saul and King David's leadership it was the same. Israel and Amalek shall never co-exist. Even to this day in Palestine the battle is still going on.

In the realm of warfare what happens in the historical church also happens in the spiritual. There is a sense in which the spiritual battle can be really exciting when understood and engaged in with the right attitude. This is so because we have started from the vantage point of assured victory, depending only on our total allegiance to the Captain of our Salvation. Look at our natural example again. 'It came to pass, when Moses held up his hand, that Israel prevailed: and when he let down his hand, Amalek prevailed'. As long as Moses kept tuned into heaven demonstrably drawing his power from the Almighty, he remained in the victory. Any loose or insecure connection resulted in power failure.

What we are saying here is that Moses had to maintain a vibrant life of prayer and supplication with thanksgiving. These times before the Lord were not going to be times of merely using words strung together as a matter of form, but utterances that were mixed with faith.

Of course, Moses was not without his vantage point, in the context that we are discussing. He had Joshua on his side, whose very name means Saviour or Deliverer. Spiritually speaking, He is the Saviour who indwells us. He is both the Conqueror and the Conquest experientially. What precious spiritual exercise it was, not only for Moses and Joshua, but also for Aaron and Hur whom we shall soon be bringing into our discussion, as bearers of the brunt of the battle.

Leaders and ministers amongst us are in mind, with reference to Hebrews 5, 'full of age', men full of the Holy Spirit who are not afraid to stand up and be counted. 'When for the time ye ought to be teachers', says verse 12 'ye have need that one teach you again which be the first principles of the oracles of God; and are become such as have need of milk, and not of strong meat'.

While the conflict lasted one aspect of assurance of continued victory was Aaron's presence. Why this man? He was very special. It was not by chance that God had chosen him to be with Moses. It is recorded in Exodus 4 that Moses baulked at the idea of being sent by God unto Pharaoh to demand the release of his people the children of Israel. '. . . and the anger of the Lord was kindled against Moses, and he said, is not Aaron the Levite thy brother? I know that he can speak well . . . and he shall be thy spokesman unto the people: and he shall be, even he shall be to thee instead of a mouth . . .' God said all this to Moses because he made the excuse that he was 'not eloquent'.

How blessedly significant this was! Spiritually speaking our natural eloquence can be a tremendous handicap. Many have made shipwreck of their own lives through over-confidence in the use of words. In a certain sense Moses was ultramodest. But God appreciated his comments, using the opportunity to bring in the Levite, Aaron. To say the least he was a vital part of the solution. His name stands for the priesthood of all believers typifying the life of ministry to God from the people, and from God to the people. He is really a sort of 'go between'.

As for Hur, he was the key to the entire battle. However important the others were he had to be numbered among them. His name means whiteness, purity, liberty.

It could well be that all of us need to be reminded more and more of Hur. If ever we are going to prevail in spiritual warfare our lives certainly need to be clean, white, and pure. How can this be? Peter helps us here. He says 'be ye holy in all manner of conversation.' And in Romans we have a reference to the Spirit of holiness. It is through His presence and activity that we become and remain holy. He would have us develop in all the attributes of the One whom He is glorifying. He would make us steadfast and sure despite the caprice that abounds all around us.

CHAPTER TWENTY

A GOOD SOLDIER

This is what Christlikeness is. Christ is formed in us. The preciousness of this is soon realized, and how heartening it is to see the names of the twelve apostles of the Lamb mentioned in Revelations 21. It is a glowing testimony to the personal handiwork of Christ displayed in such majestic setting, signifying a thoroughly completed course. The Lord is as concerned for us as ever He was for His disciples, providing opportunities for rehearsals. In the not too distant future we, like them, shall fully experience the joy of the status of being citizens of the New Jerusalem.

'He (Jesus) shall see of the travail of His soul, and shall be satisfied'. Considering this matter we are peculiarly on Holy Ground. Does not Exodus 33:21 speak of 'a place by me'? Essentially then, wherever the presence of the Lord is, that is Holy Ground. The Church of Christ is Holy. So what a privilege it is to meet in His name, knowing that His name and person are inseparable.

Note how mysteriously Joshua is introduced in Exodus 17. This is how Christ is in His people, mysterious. Joshua is just presented without any reference to his origin. God is currently creating an order of manhood who in a way is similarly mysterious, who against all odds shall be able to stand unflinchingly.

Exodus 17 really deals with us personally. It speaks of ourselves rather than of others. Here our weaknesses and our strengths are on trial. This battle with the Amalekites is concerned with our understanding ourselves. It is our proving ground where we discover how utterly dependent we must be upon the source of all strength and power. Anyone who fully realizes this is on the way to arriving at that order of things. He has already been through the experience of that man of Romans 7. He has not only met the enemy in himself, but learnt the secret of overcoming him. Having gone through that long dark tunnel as it were, and arrived in the radiance of Chapter 8, what ecstasy, what joy must fill his soul.

'There is therefore now no condemnation to them which are in Christ Jesus, who walk not after the flesh, but after the Spirit . . . for what the law could not do, in that it was weak through the flesh, God sending His own Son in the likeness of sinful flesh, and for sin, condemned sin in the flesh: that the righteousness of the law might be fulfilled in us . . .' (Rom. 8:1-3). That is where the flesh ends. God has condemned it. Where? In Christ.

In Exodus 17 Moses smote the rock. Later in Numbers 20 we see that he smote the rock twice where he should not have done so. God's commandment was that he should speak to the rock and the needed water would issue from it. What Moses did, however, denotes the absoluteness of Christ's suffering that the terror of the sin of the flesh might once and for all be thoroughly atoned for.

As we are made aware of these things our appreciation of Christ is bound to heighten. We see Joshua for who he really is. He is set against all that offends. There is no compromise in spiritual warfare and nowhere is this better shown than in Exodus 17. All the men who were chosen to fight against Amalek fought with exemplary courage. But note from the record as given in verse 13 who it was that broke the power of the enemy. It was Joshua. He 'discomfited Amalek and his people with the edge of the sword'.

The Church today has its own men and women who are being trained by the Holy Spirit in the use of the sword. We are the army of the Lord. God has not called us into His service because of who we are, but because of who He is — not because of what we can do, but what He is prepared to do through us.

Some of us are yet to change our whole way of thinking. We are yet to be delivered from thinking in our own ability, into thinking in God's. Some say God is love, that is all that matters. Paul said, if Christ had not been raised from the dead we would still have been in our sins. God save us from spiritual lethargy. He would have us 'prepared unto every good work' (2 Tim. 2:21) 'thoroughly furnished unto all good works' (2 Tim. 3:17) 'perfect in every good work' (Heb. 13:21) 'abound to every good work' (2 Cor. 9:8).

These good works are all such as He has already prepared for us to be engaged in. As God's army we are equipped for being in armed combat with the enemy day or night.

Some of us have been on the road a long time and have not shown much promise of being useful in God's army. But take courage, God is not finished with any of us yet. He wants to raise us all up in the power of His Spirit, as we yield to Him. We are coming into a wonderful new inheritance through a covenant relationship. He has given us His Word, that abiding

Word which we have believed. As we have seen before the activities of the people of God are not usually blazoned across the headlines of the world's news-papers. Nor are they often reported on the radio or television. We are nevertheless mighty through God. On our knees before Him we can open prison doors. We can set the prisoner free. We can undo the works of the enemy. All we are required to do is to be faithful.

Acts 2 helps us here. Verses 41-2 say "Then they that gladly received his (Paul's) words were baptized . . . and they continued stedfastly in the apostles' doctrine and fellowship, and in breaking of bread, and in prayers'.

The words 'they continued stedfastly' stand out with emphatic clarity, as a signal of intent, reminiscent of Moses' upheld hand. We need this Holy Ghost stamina and determination to overcome; lest our warfare be carnal rather than spiritual. Results count, and are soon manifest. In that our enemy never gives up, we cannot be neutral. Suppose a general going into battle has a thousand men and plunging in he reaps a tremendous victory, as the enemy is routed. Then at the end he counts up his men but finds that his ranks are greatly depleted.

There is, however, another general who goes in with an equal number and at the end he also counts up, and finds that he has more than he had at the beginning. Why? He was not fighting a carnal but a spiritual battle. We need not suffer loss from any attack. 'Our loss is dross'. We can be successful in all our battles as Moses was in his. It is all a matter of dedication and fullness of committment. Surely a good soldier is one who is dedicated to warfare. He knows it is not an easy life, but regardless of all the odds this is his career. It is a life that demands a great amount of discipline — of self-denial and sacrifice.

The second book of Timothy chapter 2 is written to the young man on these lines. It is a letter of encouragement, with a fatherly exhortation from Paul to receive strength from the grace 'that is in Christ Jesus'. This was the last letter of that great apostle now in prison for the second time.

Regarding Timothy, his son in the faith, as a soldier of the Cross of Christ, Paul tries to cheer him up with these words 'Thou therefore endure hardness, as a good soldier of Jesus Christ. No man that warreth entangleth himself with the affairs of this life; that he may please Him who hath chosen him to be a soldier'. Now what did Paul mean by this?

We have no right to worldliness. A man of the Spirit sets his affections on the things of the Spirit-things above; where Christ is. Paul was no 'kill joy'. Neither was he a 'spoil sport', but his word to Timothy, as to all of us, was that we cannot afford to be parleying with the world, lest we jeopardise our stance in Christ. His personal testimony was 'I press toward the mark for the prize of the high calling of God in Christ Jesus' (Phil. 3:14).

Some of us tend to look on the black side. Timothy seemed to dread the future. He was obviously upset with the general trends and situations around him, possibly like some of us are today. Discerning this, Paul encourages him by saying something like this. Though I may never see you on earth again, I want you to realize that you can be radiant, full of joy and demonstrably in victory despite anything that happens around you. You can be really full of the joy of the Lord at all times. When everyone else is going into recession you can be having a reflation — revival.

There is so much around which would overwhelm us with discouragement. Some see the state of the Church and are plunged into gloom and despondency, but there is no need of this. Others do not even know that a Christian should be joyful, and if we are, they think we must be backsliding. But we ought really to be looking up.

Of course, it is no good just saying to ourselves that we will be joyful, and then profess to be. Joyfulness comes, as we saw in Chapter eleven, when we are right with the Lord and in our own spirit. This is quite spontaneous.

It is amazing too, how many are looking for blessing. Some will travel hundreds of miles for what they think they need. But the Bible shows us that that is unnecessary. 'Blessed are they that love righteousness'. The real trouble is that many are not turning to the Bible to find out about God. They no longer go to church and all they know of God and all they see of Him is what they see in us. Consequently many people today will not respond to preaching or any other ministry. They are damned by the lives of some of us with whom they have been in contact, often in places where as Christians we had no right to be. This is a tragic indictment upon the lives of many a would-be witness unto the Lord. Spiritually they have wrecked their own future, having denied the faith.

God save us from aping the world. We do not belong to it, and should be different. So let us all by prayer and faithfulness maintain the status quo, advancing on our knees before God.

Throughout his letter to Timothy, Paul outlines the Christian pathway. He very pointedly illustrates that as soldiers it is incumbent upon us to be separated unto God. In all our duties we are related to Him loyally and responsibly. He could have taken us to heaven when we were first saved. But no; He has chosen a different way. He is training us down here for our future home. Most good parents can easily identify with this. No doubt they can afford almost anything their children ask of them, but they decline. Not because they are unkind or inconsiderate. They allow their children to learn to earn for themselves. Within reason, they give them the opportunity to suffer some privation, which is character forming.

This is what happens to those who discover the secret of steadfast praying — of drawing on God's power. Their victories over situations and circumstances cannot be equalled. They are purified by the presence of their Maker. Their thoughts are heavenly and so is their character; and appearance. How clearly the Scriptures bear this out.

Look at what happened to Jesus when He prayed. Luke 9:29 says 'the fashion of his countenance was altered, and his raiment was white and glistering'. Desiring to be Christlike, ought we not to emulate Him? The apostle Paul knew this secret well. So he helps us in 1 Thessalonians 5:17 with a crisp, pertinent exhortation, 'Pray without ceasing'. He had the right without any sense of apology to use such words. What tremendous effect prayer must have had on his life and ministry.

Do not run away. Do not be a deserter when the going is rough and difficult. It is not meant to be any easier, so do not jump out of the frying pan into the fire! Endure hardness as a good soldier, Paul would say to us.

What a marvellous thing it is to see men and women who are not entangled with the affairs of the world in these days of pressure when so many are enmeshed in the rat race. They are like glittering signposts erected by the Creator Himself. And where are they pointing? To the way of peace — of blessed assurance; of 'joy unspeakable and full of glory'. They are not going to succumb to the hustling and bustling and worldly pursuits. Their spirits are tender. They are radiant, and their hearts are in tune with heaven.

God working with them, His Word is in their heart, and His Spirit is upon them to declare it. By fervent effectual prayer they are ever in victory, sustained in power and authority by the freshness that the baptism in the Holy Spirit imparts to their lives.

God is truly revitalizing His people, infusing them with the ability to be adequate for any and every exigency. We cannot be a Moses, or a Joshua, they were for their own time: but as we apply our hearts to the service of God the Holy Spirit will teach us all we need to know and become.

God wants us to mature and therefore be able for anything through Him. 1 John 3:7 (Amp. Bible) speaks of practicing. This is really the same as we have been considering in Hebrews. 'He that practices righteousness is righteous'. Surely this is to say we ought to so familiarize ourselves with the things of God that they are thoroughly manifested in our character. Let us be 'giving thanks always for all things unto God and the Father in the name of our Lord Jesus Christ' for the end is not yet. The best is yet to be.

When David came fresh from the fields where he had been minding the sheep he had already had an encounter with the lion and the bear. He had proved his God and was showing great signs of maturity. Like David our maturity as we progress spiritually must be manifest. We must be found stepping out of our natural behaviour into the supernatural.

Who in his right mind is going to tackle a wild bear? Can we think of any sane person who would be found running after a lion that has taken a sheep or two from his farm? No matter how highly we value the sheep our own life is more precious.

David's action as a shepherd illustrates that in God we do not think of our own life. That is already in safekeeping. 'For' says Colossians 3:3 'ye are dead, and your life is hid with Christ in God'. Does this not explain why the Devil has a hard time finding us? Remember, David came to the Philistine Goliath in the name of the Lord. And what is the name of the Lord? — 'a strong tower', a hiding place. When we by faith lay hold of this way of living the enemy is not difficult to handle.

We gather from the David and Goliath episode that Goliath didn't really see his protagonist for he was 'in the tower'. A person chosen by God for any ministry needs both to know where he is and to be sure of the resources that are available to him.

As we have already noted Elisha was well aware of his own calling and he was not going to be like anybody else, not even like his master great though he was. So he did the only sensible thing by asking for a double portion of his spirit. 'He that asks receives' says Jesus. Some of us ask of God, but how much? — very little indeed, because our vision of Him is far too small. If God is for us that is all that really matters.

We do not have to be over-concerned about the enemy in difficult situations. He is only there to be overcome by us. Isn't it significant that David overcame and slew that enemy, the bear, with his bare hands? They were made for the job. This man was just being himself in God. He did not have to specially pray as to whether he might tackle the enemy. He simply did it. Realizing his resources he was in victory.

This is clearly not the time to let the enemy ride rough-shod over us. The darkness is all around us, but why should we be encumbered by the darkness. We have the light within — the Light of the Glorious Gospel of our wonderful Saviour, Jesus Christ. If we are not experiencing this already, is this not the time for reaching out to God? To be filled with the Spirit is Divine. To walk in the Spirit is Heavenly. To live in the Spirit is Christlike.